NATIONAL ACADEMIES Sciences Engineering Medicine

NATIONAL ACADEMIES PRESS
Washington, DC

Taking Stock of Science Standards Implementation

Erin Hammers Forstag, *Rapporteur*

Board on Science Education

Proceedings of a Virtual Summit

THE NATIONAL ACADEMIES PRESS 500 Fifth Street, NW Washington, DC 20001

This activity was supported by a contract between the National Academy of Sciences and the Bill & Melinda Gates Foundation (INV-005658) and the President's Committee. Any opinions, findings, conclusions, or recommendations expressed in this publication do not necessarily reflect the views of any organization or agency that provided support for the project.

International Standard Book Number–13: 978-0-309-68807-9
International Standard Book Number–10: 0-309-68807-8
Digital Object Identifier: https://doi.org/10.17226/26549

Additional copies of this publication are available for sale from the National Academies Press, 500 Fifth Street, NW, Keck 360, Washington, DC 20001; (800) 624-6242 or (202) 334-3313; http://www.nap.edu.

Printed in the United States of America

Suggested citation: National Academies of Sciences, Engineering, and Medicine. (2022). *Taking Stock of Science Standards Implementation: Proceedings of a Virtual Summit.* Washington, DC: The National Academies Press. https://doi.org/10.17226/26549.

The **National Academy of Sciences** was established in 1863 by an Act of Congress, signed by President Lincoln, as a private, nongovernmental institution to advise the nation on issues related to science and technology. Members are elected by their peers for outstanding contributions to research. Dr. Marcia McNutt is president.

The **National Academy of Engineering** was established in 1964 under the charter of the National Academy of Sciences to bring the practices of engineering to advising the nation. Members are elected by their peers for extraordinary contributions to engineering. Dr. John L. Anderson is president.

The **National Academy of Medicine** (formerly the Institute of Medicine) was established in 1970 under the charter of the National Academy of Sciences to advise the nation on medical and health issues. Members are elected by their peers for distinguished contributions to medicine and health. Dr. Victor J. Dzau is president.

The three Academies work together as the **National Academies of Sciences, Engineering, and Medicine** to provide independent, objective analysis and advice to the nation and conduct other activities to solve complex problems and inform public policy decisions. The National Academies also encourage education and research, recognize outstanding contributions to knowledge, and increase public understanding in matters of science, engineering, and medicine.

Learn more about the National Academies of Sciences, Engineering, and Medicine at **www.nationalacademies.org.**

Consensus Study Reports published by the National Academies of Sciences, Engineering, and Medicine document the evidence-based consensus on the study's statement of task by an authoring committee of experts. Reports typically include findings, conclusions, and recommendations based on information gathered by the committee and the committee's deliberations. Each report has been subjected to a rigorous and independent peer-review process and it represents the position of the National Academies on the statement of task.

Proceedings published by the National Academies of Sciences, Engineering, and Medicine chronicle the presentations and discussions at a workshop, symposium, or other event convened by the National Academies. The statements and opinions contained in proceedings are those of the participants and are not endorsed by other participants, the planning committee, or the National Academies.

Rapid Expert Consultations published by the National Academies of Sciences, Engineering, and Medicine are authored by subject-matter experts on narrowly focused topics that can be supported by a body of evidence. The discussions contained in rapid expert consultations are considered those of the authors and do not contain policy recommendations. Rapid expert consultations are reviewed by the institution before release.

For information about other products and activities of the National Academies, please visit www.nationalacademies.org/about/whatwedo.

PLANNING COMMITTEE FOR TAKING STOCK OF SCIENCE STANDARDS IMPLEMENTATION: A SUMMIT

Maya M. Garcia (*Chair*), Science Content Specialist, Colorado Department of Education
Aneesha Badrinarayan, Learning Policy Institute
James Blake, Director of Strategic Initiatives and Focus Programs, Lincoln Public Schools, Nebraska
Ravit Golan Duncan, Rutgers University
Jessica Henderson-Rockette, Instruction Partners
Victor Sampson, University of Texas at Austin
Sam Shaw, EdReports.org
Tricia Shelton, National Science Teaching Association

Amy Stephens, *Study Director*, Board on Science Education
Matthew Lammers, *Program Coordinator*, Board on Science Education (until October 2021)
Lauren Ryan, *Senior Program Assistant*, Board on Science Education (starting November 2021)
Heidi Schweingruber, *Director*, Board on Science Education

Acknowledgments

This Proceedings of a Virtual Summit was reviewed in draft form by individuals chosen for their diverse perspectives and technical expertise. The purpose of this independent review is to provide candid and critical comments that will assist the National Academies of Sciences, Engineering, and Medicine in making each published proceedings as sound as possible and to ensure that it meets the institutional standards for quality, objectivity, evidence, and responsiveness to the charge. The review comments and draft manuscript remain confidential to protect the integrity of the process.

We thank the following individuals for their review of this proceedings: Ellen Ebert, Learning and Teaching, Office of the Superintendent of Public Instruction, Washington, and Michael Heinz, Office of Standards, Division of Teaching and Learning Services, New Jersey Department of Education.

Although the reviewers listed above provided many constructive comments and suggestions, they were not asked to endorse the content of the proceedings nor did they see the final draft before its release. The review of this proceedings was overseen by Okhee Lee, Steinhardt School of Culture, Education, and Human Development, New York University. She was responsible for making certain that an independent examination of this proceedings was carried out in accordance with standards of the National Academies and that all review comments were carefully considered. Responsibility for the final content rests entirely with the rapporteur and the National Academies.

Contents

APPENDIXES

1

Introduction

On October 14 and 15, and December 8, 2021, the Board on Science Education at the National Academies of Sciences, Engineering, and Medicine held a virtual Summit entitled *Taking Stock of Science Standards Implementation*. The Summit, said Taunya Nesin (Bill & Melinda Gates Foundation), was designed to take stock of the implementation of state science standards and to determine the next steps for continuing or re-invigorating implementation efforts. Through three days of presentations and conversations, said Nesin, stakeholders will consider implementation across *all* states and territories, identify successes and challenges, and identify areas where additional resources or work is needed. The goal by the end of the Summit, she said, is for attendees to understand the current state of science standards implementation; identify what needs to happen in the next phase of implementation; and identify the tools, resources, and capital needed to advance a more just, equitable, and inclusive learning experience for our youth, teachers, and communities. (See Box 1-1 for Statement of Task.)

"Transformations in the way that science is taught across the country are under way," added Maya Garcia (Colorado Department of Education). These changes have been shaped primarily by *A Framework for K–12 Science Education* (the *Framework*) (NRC, 2012) and the Next Generation Science Standards (NGSS) (NGSS Lead States, 2013). Garcia noted that many other studies and publications have informed the work being done, including *Developing Assessments for the Next Generation Science Standards* (NRC, 2014); *Guide to Implementing the Next Generation Science Standards* (NRC, 2015); *Design, Selection, and Implementation of Instructional Materials for the Next Generation Science Standards* (NASEM,

BOX 1-1
Statement of Task

The National Academies of Sciences, Engineering, and Medicine, in partnership with the Council of State Science Supervisors, will plan and execute a public summit to take stock of the status of the implementation of the Next Generation Science Standards (NGSS) and determine the next steps possible to continue and even accelerate implementation. The proposed summit will serve as a setting to consider the implementation of the NGSS across all of the states and territories, identify successes and challenges, and identify areas were additional resources or work is needed.

The workshop committee will define the specific topics to be addressed, develop the agenda, and select and invite speakers and other participants. After the workshop, proceedings of a workshop of the presentations and discussions at the workshop will be prepared by a designated rapporteur in accordance with institutional guidelines.

2018); *Science and Engineering for Grades 6–12* (NASEM, 2019); and *Science and Engineering in Preschool Through Elementary Grades: The Brilliance of Children and The Strengths of Educators* (NASEM, 2022). As states and districts move forward with changes, this Summit presents a unique opportunity to convene as a group and reflect on the key principles and approaches that are guiding the implementation of *Framework*-based science standards. At this moment in time, said Garcia, states and districts may be feeling "implementation fatigue," along with fatigue related to the COVID-19 pandemic. It is hoped, she said, that the conversations during the Summit will "renew your efforts." The insights generated by the Summit "will generate a wave of momentum and collaboration" to support the field and communities moving forward with implementation.

The Summit planning committee process, said Garcia, began with a virtual listening tour to generate the big areas of interest; they also examined the reports listed above to identify themes across recommendations and insights from multiple sectors and stakeholders. The workshop was designed to explore the strategies and tools that communities are using to enact *Framework*-based standards, to engage with researchers and practitioners, and to reflect on the current landscape. Community engagement will continue through the spring of 2022, said Garcia, and a final workshop will be held to review what was learned and to plan the next steps as a community.

The committee used the *Framework* as a grounding point for the Summit, said Garcia, and planned the agenda and topics around its principles for implementation:

- Attend to coherence across levels, across grades, and across different components of the system.
- Attend to what is unique about science.
- Develop and provide continuing support for leadership in science at the state, district, and school levels.
- Build and leverage collaborations, networks, and partnerships.
- Take enough time to implement well.
- Make equity a priority.
- Ensure that communication is ongoing and relevant.

The planning committee pulled out two elements of these principles as a particular focus for the Summit: equity and coherence. In the 10 years since the *Framework* was released, the collective understanding around equity has evolved, said Garcia. Summit panelists were encouraged to explore how implementation efforts are making equity a priority and to provide specific examples, but they were challenged to avoid using equity as a catchall phrase. Second, the Summit is focused on how aligned and coherent efforts are key to implementation of three-dimensional science standards. For both topics, said Garcia, the Summit participants were asked to consider where there have been successes and where efforts have been constrained. Finally, the planning committee aimed to invite a wide range and diversity of voices to the table. The panels reflect a balance of practitioner and research voices across multiple sectors, said Garcia; the goal is to bring together voices from different areas and fields.

STRUCTURE OF SUMMIT AND PROCEEDINGS

The Summit took place virtually over three days, with each day featuring a combination of presentations, panel discussions, and question and answer sessions. This proceedings follows the structure of the Summit. Chapters 2 through 4 cover the first day of the Summit, with discussions on the vision of the *Framework* and the NGSS, the landscape of science standards implementation across all states, and the role of leadership. Chapters 5 and 6 cover the second day and focus on the student experience and teacher professional learning. The final panels of the workshop, held on Day 3, are summarized in Chapters 7 and 8, covering instructional materials and systems of assessment. Also on the third day, workshop participants divided into breakout groups to discuss tools and resources in different areas; the summaries of these discussions are in Chapter 9. Finally, Chapter 10 contains reflections and next steps for the field. This proceedings has been prepared by the workshop rapporteur as a factual summary of what occurred at the workshop. The planning committee's role was limited to planning and convening the workshop. The views contained in the proceedings are those of individual workshop participants and do not necessarily represent the views of all workshop participants, the planning committee, or the National Academies of Sciences, Engineering, and Medicine.

2

From Vision to Reality

Around 2008, national leaders in education began discussing the need for new science standards, said Heidi Schweingruber (Board on Science Education [BOSE]). A committee of 18 experts was convened by the National Academies to develop a *Framework for K–12 Science Education* (hereafter referred to as the *Framework*; NRC, 2012). The committee received input from four design teams, said Schweingruber, as well as feedback from thousands of educators and other stakeholders in science education. Following the committee's report, the NGSS were developed through a collaborative effort that included 26 partner states, Achieve, the National Academies, the American Association for the Advancement of Science, and the National Science Teaching Association. This process was a community effort, said Schweingruber, with input from "an amazing array of people." Schweingruber emphasized that the standards and the *Framework* be considered "living things" that are informed by the work as the field of education moves forward.

The panelists in this session of the workshop represent people who have worked with the *Framework* and the NGSS at different times and in different roles, and who have been connected to some of the many BOSE projects described by Garcia.[1] Schweingruber noted that choosing panelists for the session was challenging, as there were "thousands of people" who could have offered unique and relevant perspectives. Schweingruber moderated the discussion by posing a series of questions to the panelists and then

[1] Panelists have been involved in several different BOSE activities. Each panelist was asked to represent one of the activities, noted as part of their affiliation.

allowing Summit participants to ask questions in the chat box. The session featured four panelists:

- Philip Bell: professor of education at University of Washington; committee member for *A Framework for K–12 Science Education* (NRC, 2012); principal investigator for Advancing Coherent and Equitable Systems of Science Education project for implementation
- Elizabeth A. (Betsy) Davis: professor of education at University of Michigan; chair of the committee for *Science and Engineering in Preschool through Elementary Grades: The Brilliance of Children and the Strengths of Educators (Brilliance and Strengths)* (NASEM, 2022); co-investigator on a research project on NGSS implementation
- Michael Lach: Assistant Superintendent of Curriculum, Instruction, and Assessment at Township High School District 113; former high school science teacher; committee member for *Science and Engineering for Grades 6–12* (NASEM, 2019); worked with Achieve on the NGSS
- Tiffany Neill: Deputy Superintendent of Curriculum and Instruction at Oklahoma State Department of Education; former high school science teacher; committee member for *Call to Action for Science Education: Building Opportunity for the Future* (NASEM, 2021); former president of the Council of State Science Supervisors

THE VISION

During the early work developing the Framework, what were your hopes for what the vision and standards could accomplish? What was most exciting about the vision of the Framework?

Bell began the discussion by saying that what motivated him was to "see how far we could actually move science" education toward what is known about how people learn science. Bell's research centers on sociocultural and sociocognitive perspectives of learning, and he noted that science learning is fundamentally a cultural process. The cultural significance and relevance of the subject matter is fundamental to learner engagement and scientific literacy as learners engage with the natural world. The *Framework*, he said, highlighted the fact that science learning is cultural, and explored three dimensions of how to put this into practice in science teaching and learning. First, it is critical to build upon prior interest and identity, just as educators build on prior knowledge. Second, community cultural "funds of knowledge" can be leveraged to make connections with the subject matter. Third, educators need to leverage the diverse cultural and linguistic assets that learners bring with them to create inclusive and meaningful educational experiences. Together, these practices can open up the possibility to position learners as "knowers and doers" who can apply science education in ways that are meaningful to themselves and their communities, Bell concluded. Davis concurred and added that the *Framework* sets high yet realistic expectations for children; it views children as capable of exploring questions and solving problems that are meaningful for them, yet at the same time acknowledges that "kids are kids."

Before the *Framework* was released, said Neill, the National Academies published *America's Lab Report* (NRC, 2006), which outlined science learning goals for educators. At the time, Neill was a high school science teacher, and while the report had powerful ideas, she wondered how they could actually be implemented. For example, the report described the concept of integrated laboratory experiences, in which laboratory activities are integrated with other science learning activities such as intentional discourse and reading. When Neill read the *Framework* in 2011, she realized "this is the how." Neill viewed the *Framework* as "something big" that could help stakeholders—including rural teachers, district leaders, policy makers, and researchers—connect and move together toward a united vision of science education. Lach added that these reports and others highlight the fact that communities, educators, and other stakeholders can work together to make things better for children; he said that this is "incredibly difficult and humbling work" but is worth "dedicating our lives to."

SUCCESSES IN ADOPTION AND IMPLEMENTATION

> *What have you been most pleased about as you've watched adoption and implementation of the Framework and the NGSS unfold? What are some concrete examples of positive impact?*

The *Framework* and the NGSS, said Neill, laid out a vision for science education that gives "goosebumps." When the *Framework* and the NGSS were first developed, she said, there was a synergy of efforts to advance the vision by engaging teachers and leaders in professional learning. Teachers were trying to understand the vision and what it could look like in the classroom, and there were multiple opportunities for educators to engage with the vision and with other stakeholders to experience those "goosebump moments." The *Framework* and the NGSS also brought resources to an area—science—that had historically been underresourced, said Neill;

the national push for a coordinated vision made professional development and professional supports freely available for educators. Davis added that in addition to new professional development opportunities for in-service educators, the *Framework* and NGSS also brought opportunities for preservice teachers to think about and engage in science teaching in a way that is fundamentally different. It has been "incredibly powerful" as a teacher educator, said Davis, to see shifts in the way that preservice teachers are engaging with children.

In addition, said Neill, the *Framework* and the NGSS have disrupted the way that teachers and leaders think about students' capabilities in science. For example, Bell came to Oklahoma several years ago to work with elementary teachers. He discussed the idea of using formative assessments that resonate with the interests and identities of students; allowing students to share in their own way can open opportunities to see how students are thinking. Teachers in this professional development session became "very emotional," said Neill, because they recognized how their previous practices had been limiting their students for years. Davis followed up on this point, noting that there is considerable evidence around what children can do at young ages. The recent report on science education in preschool and elementary school (NASEM, 2022), she said, demonstrates that even 3- and 4-year-old children are capable of sophisticated learning through play. For example, a water table allows children to explore disciplinary core ideas around water and water flow, crosscutting concepts around cause and effect and systems thinking, and science practices such as investigation and using data to construct explanations.

The *Framework* and the NGSS, said Lach, acknowledge that science is "special and different"; the standards are three-dimensional, so there is a different way of looking at science than is done for other disciplines. These efforts have put science at the table in a way that it wasn't before and show that "science matters." In addition, the development of the *Framework* and the NGSS pulled together a team of teachers, administrators, and leaders who are dedicated to working together. Bell agreed and said that he is gratified to see the energy and creativity of people coming together to bring the vision into place over time; he noted that the implementation of the *Framework* can be viewed as an organic social movement, which is difficult to achieve in the space of mandated educational standards. Bell gave two examples of how science educators are helping children think critically and solve problems rather than simply memorize content. First, a third-grade classroom in Seattle has been bringing a social justice focus to the development of mass transit systems by centering the interests of communities of Black, Indigenous, and other people of color as well as the potential impacts on the ecosystem. Second, Bell shared the story of a high school biology teacher who has engaged youth in an interdisciplinary investigation into local environmental racism and the sources and impacts of pollutants. It is "amazing" to see educators using the *Framework* to build science curriculum centered on social justice, he said.

CHALLENGES IN IMPLEMENTATION

> *Where are some of the sticking points or challenges in implementation of science standards based on the Framework, and are there ways to accelerate progress?*

Forty-four states have adopted either the NGSS or standards that are inspired by the *Framework*, said Schweingruber. However, she said, implementation is different than adoption. She asked panelists to comment on where the sticking points are between adoption and implementation. Davis responded that one major challenge is that science is not prioritized in elementary schools. Science and engineering receive less instructional time than language arts and math, and this is exacerbated in schools that serve more students and communities of color. Lach agreed with this challenge and added several others: a shortage of good teachers, insufficient professional development opportunities, and a lack of quality assessments. These "have been sticking points for 20 or 30 or 50 years," he said, and there is a need for the community to consider why changes haven't happened. Another challenge, said Lach, is that there is very little overlap between the set of people who know what quality science education looks like in the classroom and the set of people who know how to run a school or school system. "We perpetuate that small overlap at our peril," said Lach, and until this gap is bridged, it will continue to be a sticking point. In addition, he said, there is a tension between being true to the standards and being true to the students. Lach said that he has seen people prioritizing strict alignment to the NGSS rather than acknowledging the role that context, nuance, and history of a school play in shaping science education to the needs of the students.

Another challenge, said Davis, is that some teachers find it difficult to build upon children's cultural and linguistic backgrounds, and to value the resources and ways of knowing that children bring to the table. Both preservice and in-service teachers, she said, need support around leveraging diversity and working toward equity and justice. She noted that the *Brilliance and Strengths* report made several recommendations in this area. First, curriculum developers work in partnership with others to develop materials that explicitly work toward equity and justice, and state and district leaders ensure that schools have access to these materials. Second, teacher educators need to foreground issues of equity in teacher education experiences; schools have a responsibility to ensure that teacher educators are prepared to do this work. Finally, said Davis, federal agencies need to fund research and development in this space to move it forward. Bell commented that these recommendations speak to the "deep structural problems and complexities" of the educational system itself, and the need to shift the existing systems and formal accountability structures. Bell shared the results from a survey of 650 science education stakeholders illustrating how they spend their time doing equity work (Bell, Campanella, and Rhinehart, 2022) (see Figure 2-1).[2] The survey found that 60 to 80 percent of these stakeholders are engaged in using meaningful phenomena, diverse sense-making, and place-based science education. He noted that about half utilize cultural pedagogies in implementation; however, racial justice and disrupting ableism are not pervasive practices and are areas for deeper growth.

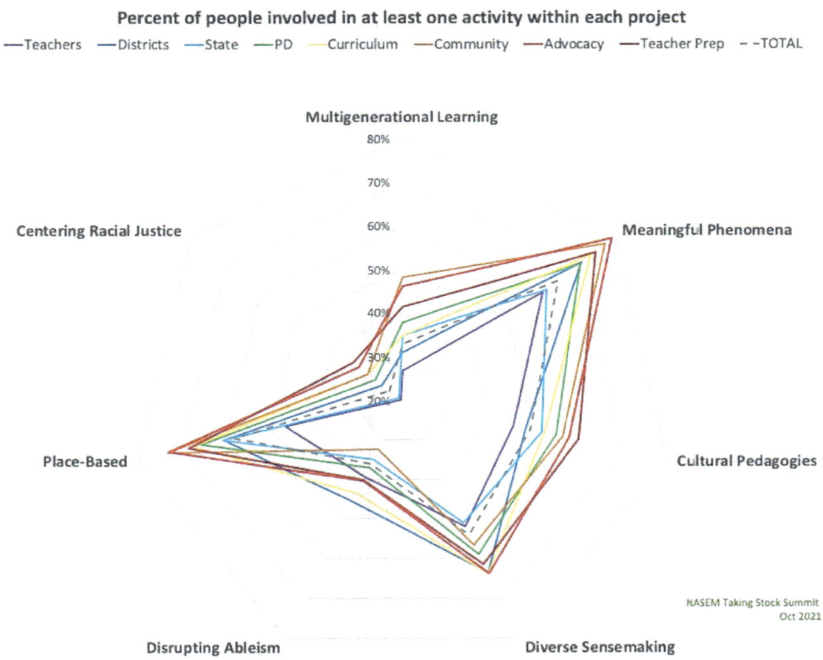

FIGURE 2-1 ACESSE National Survey of Science Education Equity Implementation.
SOURCE: Bell, Campanella, and Rhinehart (2022).

[2] These data come from the National Science Foundation-funded ACESSE (Advancing Coherent and Equitable Systems of Science Education) project.

Bell said that some have critiqued the NGSS for not centering equity. He said that Alberto Rodriguez (2015) suggested an approach of creating a fourth dimension around engagement, equity, and diversity. Bell said that he worries that equity is a jumping off point, rather than the centering focus, in much of the implementation work being conducted. He gave two examples of exceptions to this rule. First, the state science supervisor in Washington, Ellen Ebert, has "systematically built a bridge" with the Native Education Office; this sustained effort to coordinate across agencies has resulted in improved science education opportunities for Indigenous youth. Second, Mary Margaret Welch of Seattle Public Schools is building a deep partnership with a department focused on supporting emergent multilingual youth; this partnership has opened up possibilities for science-specific collaboration. These types of efforts are needed across the country, he said, but are difficult and require a lot of energy.

"Change takes time," said Neill. While the *Framework* and the NGSS have been enormously impactful over the past 10 years, it is crucial that the community "stay the course" to see widescale implementation of the vision. Many teachers have not yet had the opportunity or the support that they need to be part of the conversation, which means that "hundreds or thousands of students" also miss out on the opportunities presented by the vision. Neill urged Summit participants to commit to "not leaving a teacher behind," and noted that this process is a marathon, not a sprint. Neill also urged stakeholders to get involved in policy, whether at the district, state, or federal level. For example, teacher certification standards are being lowered in many states, which will lead to teachers coming into the profession without a strong background in science or science education. It is critical, said Neill, that stakeholders are able to articulate and advocate for the standards, funding, and professional development that are required to fulfill the vision of the *Framework* and the NGSS.

NEW CONSIDERATIONS

> *It has been almost 10 years since the Framework and the NGSS were developed; are there new opportunities or realities in the landscape that should be considered as we move forward?*

One area that has shifted since the publication of the *Framework* and the NGSS, said Davis, is our understanding of how science can effectively be integrated with other subject areas. Educators worried that integration would mean "losing what is special about science." However, evidence has accrued that integration can be an effective approach; the *Brilliance and*

Strengths report identified three evidence-based opportunities for integrating science and engineering with language arts, and two opportunities for integrating with math. This approach is particularly relevant for elementary teachers, said Davis, because they typically teach all subject areas in a self-contained classroom. Despite the benefits of this approach, there is a lack of resources to implement integration, including a lack of curriculum and materials, and challenges with the design of the school day.

Another area that has changed over the past decade, said Bell, is our understanding of equity in science education. A broad community has long been working to center ideas of equity, and the racial reckoning that has been unfolding since the death of George Floyd served as a catalyst for this transition. Bell said that he is heartened by the work being done around solidarity-based partnerships; the centering of Black, Indigenous, and other people of color family and community interests; and educational transformation. While these efforts are still not widespread, there have been "great developments in that direction."

LESSONS LEARNED

> *As we move forward to further enact this vision, what advice can you share? What are the lessons you have learned about successful implementation?*

Panelists shared their lessons learned from the past 10 years of work on implementing the vision of the *Framework* and the NGSS. These insights included the following:

- Intellectual and trusting relationships between stakeholders are the foundation for implementing science education that is meaningful for students. (Bell)
- Collaboration and networks are essential for purposeful continued implementation of the vision. (Neill)
- It is critical to center the voices and interests of marginalized communities when planning educational design and implementation efforts. (Bell)
- Teacher educators, facilitators of professional learning experiences, and school and district leaders need to support teachers' efforts to teach science and engineering well. (Davis)
- Implementation is a marathon, not a sprint; allow time and support to observe how changes play out in the classroom before making further changes. (Neill and Lach)

While the *Framework* and the NGSS were national efforts, said Lach, the work of implementing the vision happens on the local level. The day-to-day relationships and the "sweat and the grit" are in classrooms, departments, and schools, he said. Schweingruber asked panelists to comment on how national leadership can ensure coherence across the system while also honoring the local nature of change and the inclusion of diverse communities in the work. Bell responded that ideally, national policy and leadership provides openings to meaningful local engagement; rather than starting with the NGSS, communities can start with the learning and use the standards as a foundation and guide. Neill added that the *Framework* and the NGSS were structured as "offerings for the learning goals that states would adopt." At the state level, adoption of standards happens through bringing committees of diverse representatives together, and at the local level, committees of teachers come together to select materials or give guidance on professional development. Of course, said Neill, these processes are not perfect, and efforts are needed to train teachers and teacher leaders to be advocates and to ensure that decisions are made with the input of a broad and diverse group of people. Bell added that making decisions that serve the local interest requires not just input from diverse and marginalized communities but working in solidarity with these communities. Lach said that while there are parts of the system that need changing because they are "inefficient and unjust," there are "limits to that kind of work." Lach urged Summit participants to consider ways to improve science education for children regardless of whether there are changes in the system, "because there are a whole bunch of kids out there that we have to do better for." Schweingruber concluded that implementing the vision of the *Framework* and the NGSS may require setting both short- and long-term goals, and that "we have to do both at once." Structural change may take years to accomplish, she said, but in the meantime, science educators can respond to the needs of communities and facilitate local action and innovation.

3

The Landscape of Implementation

In the previous session, said Garcia, panelists discussed some of the challenges of implementation (see Chapter 2). During that session, Summit participants were asked to contribute to a "word cloud" to visualize what they saw as the biggest challenges for implementation (Figure 3-1). Garcia said that some of the main challenges identified were time, professional learning, high-quality materials, time for teacher learning, teaching time, and time for professional development.

In this session of the Summit, panelists further explored the issue of implementation and shared their insights from research and practice. The session was moderated by Garcia, who led the discussion by posing questions to the panelists. There were four panelists:

- Stefanie Marshall: assistant professor at University of Minnesota; focuses on the intersection of policy, organizational leadership, and science education
- Bill Penuel: professor of learning sciences and human development at University of Colorado, Boulder; focuses on how long-term research-practice partnerships can create more equitable and coherent systems at the state and district level
- Jenny Sarna: director of NextGenScience at WestEd; former science teacher
- Jim Spillane: professor of learning and organizational change at Northwestern University; focuses on understanding efforts to support elementary science teaching that is aligned with the NGSS

FIGURE 3-1 Biggest challenges in implementation.
SOURCE: Workshop participants.

COMMUNITY

> *What is bringing together the community in ways that allow us to move forward with the vision for equitable science education, and what is challenging or constraining these efforts?*

"What is bringing people together around science education is a recognition that by not doing science we're harming people," said Marshall. When students are not offered quality science education, she said, individuals and communities are harmed—lives are literally on the line. Marshall said that a child's zip code or race should not impact their access to quality science education, and she shared a story of a girl from Flint, Michigan. While serving on a career panel, Marshall was asked a question by a Black high schooler named Faith: "How did you know you could do science?" This question, said Marshall, indicates that someone had framed Faith's reality in such a way that she didn't know that she was a "doer of science." Marshall answered, "I didn't know I couldn't." She noted that her own perspective was a privilege and that "we have a responsibility to counter the status quo" for students like Faith. Changing the status quo will require considering how power and information guides decision making, and actively disrupting the current system.

Penuel underscored these points and added that "we find ourselves in a different moment now" than 10 years ago. Penuel pointed to the COVID-19 pandemic, state legislation that bans conversations about racial equity in schools, and science being eliminated from curricula due to concerns about learning loss during the pandemic. Science education is an urgent and life-saving matter, said Penuel, but there are forces that are working against this idea. To teach science is to "enable people to live and survive in this moment," he said. In so doing, we have to focus on the distribution of opportunity and ensure that all students have access to quality science education. Many decisions about science education are made at the local level (e.g., time allocation, graduation requirements), said Penuel, and these are leverage points for intervention. Penuel urged Summit participants to stay focused on implementing the overall vision of the *Framework* and the NGSS rather than narrowly focusing on specific components.

UNIQUENESS OF SCIENCE

> *What makes implementation in science education different than implementation in language arts and math?*

One of the main differences, said Spillane, is that it is challenging to get "science taught in the first place." This is very different than language arts or math, and it is "not an accident" but is a function of a quarter-century of state and federal policies and incentives for language arts and math. Spillane shared details from his research on what rationales state science coordinators use to convince schools to teach science. Some use rationales that are instrumental, for example, that teaching science will help kids with language arts and math. Others argue that science education is necessary to ensure access for all children to STEM jobs. Still others put forth a "democratic goal" of creating an informed citizenry who can engage in pressing challenges that we face as a nation and a world, such as climate change.

Another key difference, said Sarna, is the critical role of partnerships. Science education requires resources—both physical materials and human resources—that districts struggle to provide. External partners can play a role in bringing these resources into communities and supporting educators and leaders on their implementation journey, she said. When partners connect with communities, bring educators together, and focus on real needs, "that collaboration is so much greater" than what could happen in one district alone. Sarna shared examples of external partners from across the country, from the Museum of Science and Industry in Chicago to UC Boulder in Colorado, and said that these partners can provide tools, resources, and professional learning opportunities. She noted that while these partnerships are usually local, the resources and information can be shared with educators and leaders across the country.

A Summit participant asked for panelists to comment on how access to these types of partnerships can be improved for schools such as those that are geographically isolated or difficult-to-staff schools that serve historically marginalized students. Penuel gave an example of improving access for rural schools; he said that Colorado is developing supports for an online professional learning course for teachers in rural areas that focuses on five-dimensional science assessment. Marshall added that when school leaders and principals have a strong vision for science education, they reach out to the community and make necessary connections. She cautioned, however, that schools be deliberate about the organizations they partner with, particularly when money is used to direct science education in a specific direction—the direction may not be desirable, equitable, or sustainable.

EQUITY IN RESOURCES

How can resource sharing help improve equitable access to quality and coherent science education?

In response to this question, Penuel shared details about his work on the Advancing Coherent and Equitable Systems of Science Education (ACESSE) project.[1] ACESSE focuses on building coherent systems horizontally and vertically, around an equitable vision for science education. Penuel explained that the vision includes the three dimensions from the NGSS, along with deep attention to the interests, identities, and experiences of students, particularly those from non-dominant groups and communities. Horizontal coherence means that professional learning assessments, curricula, leadership, and instructional guidance are all aligned with this vision, and vertical coherence means that people at every level of the system share a common vision.

ACESSE has developed three kinds of tools to help achieve these goals, said Penuel. The first is a set of professional learning resources that were co-designed with state and local leaders, educators, and researchers. These tools focus on leverage points for assessment and can be used to lead professional learning with other educators around the vision. The second is a

[1] http://cosss.org/ACESSE.

set of tools to support leaders in thinking about and seeing their systems. For example, one tool maps network actors (e.g., policies, people) to identify facilitators, barriers, and potential allies. The third kind of tool, said Penuel, is designed to collect data to take stock of implementation progress.

ROLE OF LEADERS

What is the role of leaders in implementation efforts?

Garcia said that as the planning committee reviewed reports about implementation of the NGSS and the *Framework*, it became clear that intentional engagement and involvement of leadership was critical for implementation. She asked panelists to comment on how they see leadership in connection with implementation efforts.

Spillane replied that this theme has existed in the implementation literature for decades, and it is not surprising that it comes up with elementary science education. A lack of leadership is one of the key challenges that state science supervisors identify; in particular, the school principal often acts as a gatekeeper to whether science gets taught. Spillane stressed, however, that leadership should not be equated solely with the school principal. There are leaders within the school, such as teacher leaders and specialist teachers, as well as leaders in the system, such as at the district office. Spillane argued for a "distributed perspective" on leadership, both looking horizontally and vertically across the system. He added that individuals beyond the formal system—such as community members—could also be engaged in and lead this work. In contrast to language arts and math, said Spillane, the leadership for science education is a vast network that operates at multiple levels and is "a social movement" mobilized to promote reform of elementary school science.

Marshall agreed that science education leadership be distributed but added that principals sometimes are left out of the conversation. Often, she said, only teachers and district-level staff are trained, and principals are unable to engage in important conversations because they are not familiar with the standards and the lingo of science education. In addition, many principals have limited experience in science, either in their education or professional development experiences. In language arts and math instruction, principals are forced to make decisions due to pressure from national, state, and local policies. These pressures are largely non-existent in science education, she said, so some principals may simply not engage in this area. Principals may also not be familiar with the resources available to them, such as science consultants at the district level.

CRITICAL NEEDS

What is the most critical need for advancing more just, equitable, and inclusive science learning experiences?

"We need to reframe how people are thinking about science," said Marshall. She said that science is underprioritized, underfunded, and under-resourced, and that we largely rationalize and accept that science is lower on the hierarchy than language arts or math. We need to advocate for science to be raised up; otherwise, it will always "be on the back burner." Spillane agreed and noted that the hierarchy in elementary education is a function both of history and of elaborate federal and state funded infrastructures that support language arts and math. Due to these infrastructures and the ongoing testing in language arts and math, there are more data with which to make decisions than there are for science. Spillane emphasized that he was not arguing for more testing but that it is important to consider how the infrastructures vary dramatically among these subject areas. Penuel followed up on this, saying that science education scholars need to do the work of "infrastructuring"—that is, redesigning the infrastructure to align with the vision of science education. For example, ACESSE works to develop rubrics for student learning assessment, to coordinate with observation protocols that are used to evaluate teachers, and to build assessments that align with the vision. The work of infrastructuring includes redesigning systems, building new structures, and, in some cases, abolishing existing systems.

ADOPTION, ADAPTATION, AND THE NEED FOR A COMMON VISION

Are there differences between states that have adopted the NGSS and those that have adapted them?

Jessica Henderson-Rockette (Instruction Partners) noted that while some states have adopted the NGSS wholesale, others have adapted the standards; she asked panelists to comment on any differences between adoption and adaption states. Sarna first responded that there is little evidence available on this issue; she observed that there would be "a lot more data" if the subject area was language arts or math. Despite the lack of evidence, it is clear that even states that have adapted their own standards based on the *Framework* and the NGSS are able to utilize many of the same tools and resources, such as open-source curricula or learning modules. Whether a state has adapted or adopted, the standards are "grounded in this common vision." The small differences in content, she said, are less consequential due to this common vision.

A Summit participant asked panelists to comment on how this common vision can be established both horizontally and vertically within a school system. Spillane said that it is "impossible" to build the infrastructure necessary to support elementary science education unless there is a shared understanding among the key partners. He noted that if "everybody has different ideas about what should be taught," it makes it very challenging to move forward. Spillane said that he has "a lot of hope" that building a shared vision is possible, due to the fact that local systems are being connected to each other and to the states through work that is happening nationally. Penuel added some data from his research on what factors make a difference in establishing a shared vision. One factor is a sense of collective efficiency—that is, that the group of people feels that they can make a difference. Progress is also easier, he said, when there are regular routines that bring together people from schools, districts, state agencies, teacher associations, communities, and other organizations. "If you have a group of people who stay the course, you can make progress," he concluded.

4

The Role(s) of Leadership

Many leaders in education, said James Blake (Lincoln Public Schools), do not have the word "leader" in their title. The work is done at a distributed level with teacher leaders, district leaders, and community members who have all embraced the leadership opportunities that are inherent to their role. In this session, Summit participants heard from leaders at different levels and in different roles. Blake guided the conversation by asking questions of each panelist, starting from the "balcony view" and drilling down into the school building.

The five panelists were as follows:

- Mike Heinz: science coordinator, New Jersey Department of Education; president of Council of State Science Supervisors
- Elizabeth Mulkerrin: Omaha Zoo and Aquarium; National Science Teaching Association president elect; former science teacher
- Gudiel Crosthwaite: superintendent, Lynwood Unified School District
- Zoe Evans: principal, Bowdon High School; former science teacher
- Takako Olson: director of curriculum, Lincoln Public Schools

CREATING A COMMON VISION OF SCIENCE WITHIN THE EDUCATION SYSTEM

How do you describe the system that impacts science education from the national level down to the classroom?

At the federal level, began Heinz, the Every Student Succeeds Act[1] (ESSA) affects budget and time in schools. Heinz shared his opinion that ESSA accidentally overemphasizes math and English language arts at the expense of science. There are many national organizations, including NSTA (National Science Teaching Association), AAAS (American Association for the Advancement of Science), CSSS (Council of State Science Supervisors), NSELA (National Science Education Leadership Association), and the National Academies, that have a great deal of influence in shaping resources and policies for educators. On the state level, governors and commissioners bring their policy ideas to the table, and state boards of education are either appointed or elected. At the mid-level of leadership, said Heinz, there are district-level superintendents, building-level administrators, supervisors, and educators. Heinz said that educators "have a lot of people standing behind them, each nudging and pushing and pulling a little bit." To communicate and establish a coherent vision of science education in this system, Heinz said that he tries to speak simply, speak without jargon, and use only a few words to state his case. Regardless of the "pushes and pulls," the message for science education has remained consistent over the past 12 years since the development of the NGSS.

Mulkerrin agreed with the need for a common vision and added that the community can be an important partner in implementing the vision. Informal science organizations, such as museums, nature centers, zoos, and aquariums, also need a place at the table to discuss how to engage students and teachers to meet the needs of the community. Crosthwaite added that organizations that hold the same vision can be critical partners in reinforcing, supporting, and guiding science education; he said that schools and educators manage many demands, so it can be enormously helpful to have partners who are able to focus more closely on science education. He emphasized, however, that partnerships be used to build capacity so that efforts are sustainable moving forward.

OPPORTUNITIES AT THE DISTRICT LEVEL

> *As a superintendent, how do you address the needs of your students regarding science?*

To open the conversation around opportunities at the district level, Crosthwaite shared information about the district he works for—Lynwood Unified School District—that serves about 12,000 students and is located

[1] https://www.ed.gov/essa?src=rn.

about 15 miles southeast of Los Angeles, California. The community is historically underserved, with nearly all students qualifying for free and reduced lunch; 94 percent of students are Latino, 5 percent are Black, and about a third are English language learners. Unfortunately, said Crosthwaite, there is a large achievement gap for English learners across the state of California; these disparities include differences in math proficiency and graduation rates. There are 4.9 million students who are English learners across the nation, and it is the fastest-growing population. "If we are serious about supporting all kids," he said, we need to ensure that we understand the demographics of students and their specific needs.

Crosthwaite shared the details of how science education was transformed in his school district. In 2010, 55 percent of the students in the district had access to biology, which was the only college-required science course offered. The district brought together teachers, students, and community members, and had "hard conversations" to decide how to best support the students. The group determined that "if we truly believe in kids," students need access to the rigorous courses that are required for college entrance. There were many barriers in the way, he said, including lack of prerequisites, low GPAs, and credentialing for educators. The district worked to find ways around these barriers, and now 97 percent of ninth-grade students and 68 percent of juniors are enrolled in college-required science courses. Crosthwaite stressed that if expectations are raised, students will rise to the challenge. Generally, when more students take advanced placement exams, the passing rate goes down; however, in Lynwood, it went slightly up when classes were opened to more students. Lynwood has been recognized for its success in improving access to rigorous courses for students of color, said Crosthwaite, and students now have a better, more well-rounded, more hands-on experience with science.

Blake asked Crosthwaite to further describe the roadmap of how these changes were implemented. Crosthwaite said it was a process that involved many conversations and meetings among principals, department chairs, and educators. These conversations involved looking closely at the data about which students had access to what types of courses, and principals were "key to these conversations." Schools developed new master schedules, and there were systems put in place to check whether the new schedules were working as intended. Blake added that master schedules are a "puzzle," but that there are programs that allow you to "stand back and look at the equity within the schedule." Crosthwaite said that one critical role of the district is to determine which school activities are non-negotiable and which are expendable. Although teachers are the experts, and deserve some autonomy in their work, districts can help make the difficult decisions about how to allocate time and resources to best support students.

ROLE OF SCHOOL LEADERS

What is the role of a school leader in the implementation of the Framework and the NGSS?

Blake asked Evans and Olson to comment on the role of school leaders in implementation of the NGSS. Evans, who is currently principal of a small, rural high school in Georgia, said that principals serve multiple roles: gatekeepers, filters, and motivators. Principals are the gatekeepers of whether and how new standards or curricula are implemented. They also serve to filter out noise and conflicting information from the community, classrooms, educators, and the district. For example, said Evans, if a science teacher wants to implement three-dimensional (3-D) teaching and learning, school-level administrators have a responsibility to help the teacher figure out the process and how to remain in compliance with relevant policies. Another role is to encourage and motivate teachers to make changes. Evans noted that some teachers are very comfortable in their teaching practices, and that doing new things is "very frightening." School-level administrators can encourage these educators to have the courage to learn new things and implement new practices to improve education for the students. Evans likened the role of principal to that of a "ringmaster" who wears "lots of hats."

Olson, who serves as the director of curriculum for Lincoln Public Schools, said that one of her jobs is to create an opportunity for educators to speak with stakeholders (e.g., superintendents and school board members) in a way that allows them to understand 3-D standards. For example, she said, educators can explain the pedagogical shift from "learning about" to "figuring out." These are important words to use to get stakeholders to buy into 3-D standards; establishing buy-in is particularly critical for stakeholders who control budgets and resources.

STUDENT-DRIVEN EDUCATION

How might we be able to make decisions based on what is in the best interest of our students?

Blake asked the panelists to consider what science education would look like if educators were "just teaching for fun" and in the best interests of their students (rather than toward standards or assessments). Mulkerrin responded that one critical piece is establishing a sense of exploration and engagement within students. To do so, educators need to be listening to what kids are talking about, what is relevant in the community, and what "science action" is happening locally. In an ideal world, educators are facilitators for students to explore things that are relevant and interesting to them, she said. In the high school program at the Omaha Zoo Academy, students take classes focused on animal science and conservation research. Within these areas of focus are the traditional subjects of English, social studies, math, and science; the particular projects and topics of study are driven by the students. Each year, the students develop a new set of questions to explore, and the teachers and staff help the students engage in these efforts to discover and learn concepts through experiential learning. The result of this approach, said Mulkerrin, is that many Zoo Academy students are following their interests and pursuing careers in science; she noted that there is now a surplus of veterinarians, veterinarian techs, and conservation researchers in the Omaha area. The 26 years of success at the Zoo Academy demonstrates the importance of letting students facilitate, guide, and direct their own learning, she said.

ADDRESSING CHALLENGES IN IMPLEMENTATION

What are the greatest needs associated with implementation?

Blake asked panelists to identify the greatest needs associated with implementation of the NGSS. Evans identified two major challenges: professional learning and high-quality materials. Professional learning "always has to come first," she said, and the need will never end. New teachers will always be entering the system, and there will always be some teachers who need support for their ambitious plans and some teachers who need more basic education and training. High-quality materials can help support teachers who are entering teaching without a strong science background or who are coming from another field. Evans said that in her experience, teachers tend to return to their "safe place," which is the way they were taught themselves. Both professional learning and high-quality materials can help these teachers make the transition from 1-D to 3-D education. Heinz encouraged cross-border collaborations and partnerships, noting that educators who work together to develop resources are at the same time getting rich professional learning opportunities. Collaboration is an "incredibly powerful tool" for educators and it helps ease the heavy lifting, Heinz said. Evans concurred with the power of collaboration and noted that as a non-NGSS state with standards that were informed by the *Framework*, Georgia is still able to use materials and resources from other states. Particularly in schools and communities where science teachers may not have colleagues, it is essential to be able to build community and share resources. This is one of the "wonderful things" that has come out of NGSS implementation, said Evans. Doors and borders were opened, and educators were able to share ideas and resources that could be modified for the needs of a particular community.

Olson added that developing good resources—such as professional learning and high-quality materials—requires ample budget allocation and prioritization of stakeholders. It can be challenging to elevate science education in a "reading and math heavy society," but it is imperative. It is critical for school districts to have a voice within their department of education, whether as consultants, collaborators, or advocates. School districts can also partner with higher education institutions that train preservice science teachers. When working with state deparments of education around curriculum assessment, educators need to place themselves in the position to "have the power to change mindset and practices."

5

Centering Student Experience in Science

The *Framework* advocates for engaging students in the *doing* of science, said Ravit Duncan (Rutgers University). The *Framework* report states that a major goal for science education is to allow students to "systematically investigate issues related to their personal and community priorities." By centering instruction on students' lived experiences, said Duncan, science education can be coherent across lessons, units, and grades. However, she said, coherence and centering student experiences are "in the eye of the beholder." Not all students feel that their experiences, knowledge, and bodies are welcome and valued in science. Duncan shared several quotes from students that illustrate this idea (Calabrese Barton and Tan, 2020, 2021; Calabrese Barton, Tan, and Birmingham, 2020):

- "When you walk into some classrooms, you feel they don't want you there." (Sana, age 13)
- "Teachers care, but they do not care about the community all of the time. We go outside on our time, and find places where we can go do science or engineering for our communities. School doesn't know how to do that. School doesn't know that we do that. We need to tell our teachers how we do it. We got to help them." (Samuel, age 14)
- "The racist stereotype is that Black people are not listening to science. But that is not true. Maybe it's the other way around, like science is not listening to us.... I want you to know how I feel as a young, Black girl in America and in STEM. I want to feel like I can be me in STEM and have that celebrated." (Jazmyn, age 15)

In thinking about the experiences of students in the classroom, said Duncan, several questions emerged during the planning of this session: Whose experiences are we centering? How and when are we centering them? Toward what end? The extent to which science learning environments are spaces in which students feel seen, heard, and valued as persons and knowledge producers depends on how we answer these questions. How equity and justice are considered day-to-day has consequences for student experiences in the classroom. To frame the discussion, Duncan shared definitions of "equity" and "justice" from the report on *Science and Engineering in Preschool through Elementary Grades* (NASEM, 2022). The committee used the term "equity" to address ways—through changing policies and practices—of removing barriers to participation in science and engineering and increasing achievement, representation, and identification, whereas the term "justice" refers to addressing systemic oppressions that cause those barriers, thus seeking fair treatment of all people and supporting opportunities for self-determination and thriving (NASEM, 2022). In this session of the Summit, Duncan asked the panelists a series of guiding questions, followed by open discussion. The five panelists were as follows:

- Edna Tan: professor at University of North Carolina at Greensboro; focuses on equitable and consequential science learning for historically underrepresented minority youth
- Rabiah Harris: eighth-grade science teacher and team lead at Ida B. Wells Middle School; 17 years experience in teaching
- Lauren Kaupp: educational specialist for science and STEM at the Hawaii Department of Education; experience in curriculum design, professional development, and standards implementation
- Maria Olivares: research assistant professor at Boston University; works in partnership to develop learning environments that support expansive and creative inquiry in STEM
- Enrique Suárez: assistant professor at University of Massachusetts, Amherst; designs learning environments that support young, emerging, multilingual students in leveraging their conceptual resources and trans-languaging practices for learning science

STUDENT PERSPECTIVES

> *What are you hearing from students about their experiences in science classrooms?*

Students' experiences in science class, said Kaupp, often boil down to a simple dichotomy: "they like the hands-on part of science class, and they don't like when science class is boring." Part of the standards implementation, she said, has been broadening teachers' understanding of what science teaching and learning looks like, and moving away from the idea of "hands-on science" toward the idea of "minds-on science." However, said Kaupp, students are telling us that they like hands-on science: they want to touch things and do things. This has always been important to students, but it particularly resonates after a year and a half of distance learning. While it is important to center students' real-life experiences in science education, said Kaupp, it is also critical to consider their experiences in the classroom itself.

Olivares added that it is essential to reflect on the purpose of teaching and learning, the purpose of scientific thinking, and the value for students in engaging in these disciplinary practices. Coming out of the pandemic, she said, there has been a "hyper focus" on learning loss. The question, however, is what did they lose, and do we want to impose that on them again? Pre-pandemic learning was not founded on nurturance, meant to uplift students, or meant to expand thinking; there is now an opportunity to rethink the purpose of learning with a longer vision. The children in our classrooms are the future, she said, and "we should be teaching them as such." Everything we do in the classroom needs grounding in the long-term vision of education rather than "triaging whatever is happening in that moment."

DIMENSIONS OF STUDENT EXPERIENCES

What are the different dimensions of centering student experience that should be under consideration as part of this Summit?

When considering how to center student experiences, said Tan, it is productive to frame the work against a backdrop of historical and systematic injustices and oppressions that have been visited on the bodies of particular groups of students disproportionately. "The past is carried in our bodies, in our ideologies, in our framings, in our positionings," and the past impacts how individuals perform in the here and now. Students in a classroom are not a homogenous group—some are from the dominant culture, whereas others are students of color, immigrants, refugees, multilingual students, or students who identify as LGBTQ+. Some students have multiple identifiers and intersecting identities and experiences that are germane to their sense of self and how they come to science learning. The question, said Tan, is whose experiences do we center, and when, and how? Tan argued that there is a need to develop guidelines to answer this question, because "when we go back to the norm," we amplify the dominant culture of white, middle class, and heterosexual. This is the norm of science education, the norm we have been entrenched in, and the norm that we know, she said.

Harris added that teachers have a duty to learn about students as individuals because "they matter," and they are a part of the community space. This can be done in many ways and different places, such as on recess duty, in conversations with parents, and in class discussions and assignments. Tan agreed and said that teachers are usually familiar with eliciting student stories and experiences as part of the exploration or framing of the phenomenon (e.g., "Have you ever encountered this in your family?"). However, she said, it often stops there, and student experiences are only used as an on-ramp to a science unit that is already mapped out. Harris said that this part is "so tricky." For science education to be centered on student experiences, it is critical for units and curricula to be given "space to breathe." That is, teachers need to be able to adjust and adapt based on what their students are bringing to the table. Teachers can be flexible in this way, said Harris, but only if administrators give them the space to do so. Tan added that centering student experiences is a paradigm shift that requires teachers to be nimble and requires administrators and staff to foster an environment of support for teachers and students.

Harris gave an example of how students' lives and experiences can be brought into the science classroom. In a unit on chemical reactions, Harris asked her students to tell her about ways that matter changed in their life (e.g., eating dinner). Her students responded that her homework was "a little weird" because she was asking them about things that happened in their day-to-day life. She said that students were "blown away" and reported that no teacher had ever really asked them to think in this way before. The more that teachers can connect topics with student experiences, the more the students will understand that they are already doing science. Olivares added another example of a middle school teacher who designed a unit on Newton's laws of motion. The students were given the assignment of making kinetic sculptures, or something that moves. The teacher asked the students to consider how social movements—such as Black Lives Matter—connect with ways of understanding motion and physics. This assignment allowed students to decide what they wanted to make, to connect science with things that were important to them, and to "author themselves" into the materials that existed within the physics course. Olivares said that this was a very enriching experience for students, with engagement, collaboration, and enjoyment without the pressure to produce a particular product or come up with a particular answer.

EQUITY

> *How do you think about the intersection between equity and centering student experience?*

"I start from the understanding," said Suárez, that while opportunities and access to resources are important parts of equity, "we cannot stop there." Suárez shared several perspectives on an equitable approach to science education. He said that an equitable approach

- centers student experiences and acknowledges, mitigates, and redresses the sociohistorical and sociopolitical oppressions of the past and the present;
- creates opportunities for self-determination and group deliberation, instead of using students' experiences only as steppingstones toward dominant knowledge and ways of knowing; and
- recognizes the value of diversity and acknowledges that "we are doing ourselves a disservice" by excluding certain people and different ways of knowing.

If we coordinate multiple ways of understanding and multiple ways of relating to the natural world, we create better knowledge. These issues, said Suárez, are systematic and systemic, and addressing them requires bringing together diverse stakeholders to create space for conversation with people "outside of our bubbles."

Olivares agreed and added that it is not enough to solicit diverse voices without sustained and meaningful engagement of stakeholders, in a way that is consequential, nurturing, and responsive. Although the need for STEM education is often framed in relation to the need for the future workforce, it is essential that we are integrating students and their needs into our systems. Nurturing the process of learning and personally meaningful experiences, she said, encourages expansive and creative thinking, which is what will be needed in the future. Olivares added that the systemic nature of inequity should push researchers to reconceptualize how they think about collaboration. As researchers, she asked, "How do we orient to our communities? Do we orient to them as fellow researchers, with a depth of knowledge and expertise that we do not have?" Collaborating with communities allows us to pool our resources and "disrupt inequity simultaneously on multiple fronts."

BARRIERS

What are the barriers to centering student experiences in science teaching and learning?

A recent survey found that only about 20 percent of teachers felt well-prepared to teach in ways that are culturally responsive and culturally sustaining, said Suárez. In addition, only about a quarter of teachers said that they attend professional development that addresses these issues. This is a barrier to centering student experiences with a focus on equity, he said. Administrators, researchers, teacher educators, and professional development providers need to be intentional about centering racial justice and making it central to the work of science education. Furthermore, it is critical to understand how ableism[1] is pervasive in how we think about science learning. Suárez noted that the phrase "hands-on learning" has a "twinge of ableism." We need to provide opportunities and resources for K–12 science educators to engage with these issues and address them. Olivares added that this can be done in ways other than in the rigid environment of traditional professional development. For example, research-practice partnerships can cultivate the knowledge and experience needed to center student experience and move science education forward.

IMPLICATIONS FOR CLASSROOMS

Given the discussions about equity and centering student experiences, what are the implications for classrooms and classroom teachers?

Tan said that equity and centering student experiences are systemic issues, and that an ecosystem lens is necessary to understand and address these issues across space and time. Tan encouraged a zoom in/zoom out approach, in which stakeholders can zoom out to see the historical and contextual nature of inequities and can zoom in to address these issues in the classroom day-to-day. She said that there is a need to upend the status quo, and that "the time is now" to find ways to address systemic oppressions and rethink the classroom. Tan shared an example of one classroom

[1]Ableism is the discrimation of and prejudice against people with disabilities based on the belief that typical abilities are superior. For more information, see https://www.accessliving.org/newsroom/blog/ableism-101/.

initiative and noted that while the issues are systemic, individual stories are "empowering and very necessary empirically to document" the efforts to disrupt the system. A partner teacher in North Carolina was developing a unit about engineering for sustainable communities. The teacher, said Tan, was a white, middle-class woman, whereas the class was extremely racially, ethnically, and linguistically diverse. The students conducted a community ethnography, with the school itself as the community. Students interviewed stakeholders, parents, and students, and identified problems such as low morale, stress, and bullying. One particular issue was bullying in the bathroom, and the students found that the small size of the stall doors was causing girls to have to contort their bodies to stay safe, or to avoid going to the bathroom altogether. The students engineered a door extender with a panel for more privacy. Tan said that while this solution may not seem "dramatic," it addressed an injustice that was preventing the girls from being functional, alert, and motivated. Trauma and injustice can be mundane yet insidious, she said, building up over time. This project made a basic human need "visible through engineering," and allowed the students to do rigorous science while being the experts and the leaders of their own community.

Kaupp added that there is a need to rethink the physical space of classrooms to better support student learning. Even before the social distancing of COVID-19 protocols, she said, science classrooms were often arranged with desks in rows all facing one direction. To facilitate the types of teaching and learning advocated for by the NGSS and the *Framework,* it is important to consider ways to rearrange the physical spaces of the classroom.

Kaupp stressed that these are systems issues, and "we can't put the full weight" on classroom teachers. Supplies, equipment, and professional development to support classroom teachers can be provided by the system, and the system can also provide resources such as videos, high-quality curricular materials, and supplemental materials. When we are asking teachers "to do a heavy lift," there is a need for the system to honor their time and treat them like the professionals they are. Olivares added that when she works with teachers, she tries to identify flexible structures rather than particulars. In contrast, the educational system tends to focus on particulars in the absence of process, deep thinking, and deep engagement. Teachers need to be allowed to be versatile and improvise within a flexible structure, she said. Suárez said that there is a need to rethink how we evaluate expertise in teachers. There is expertise at every level, and expertise in different areas, and we need to facilitate bringing teachers together to share expertise and support each other. "Throwing people into the deep end" without support is not advisable, he said, but we also need to recognize that all teachers at all levels bring an expertise that can be honored and built upon.

6

Teacher Professional Learning

Garcia opened by asking participants to vote on their most challenging instructional shifts in relation to the implementation of three-dimensional (3-D) standards (see Figure 6-1 for the percent of respondents selecting each instructional shift). Of the choices provided, 35 percent of participants selected "letting go of content coverage" was the most challenging instructional shift, followed by "supporting students' sensemaking" (23%) and "integrating 3 dimensions" (19%).

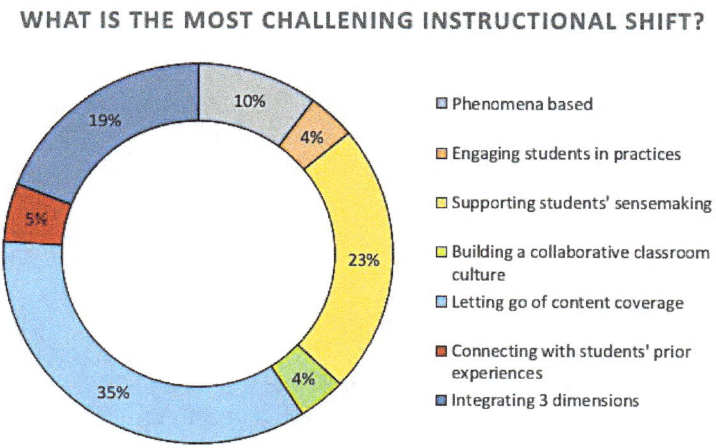

FIGURE 6-1 Participant responses during the session to a poll on what they currently perceive as the most challenging instructional shift.

Throughout the Summit, participants identified "professional learning" as a necessary component of implementing the *Framework* and the NGSS. In this session, panelists explored issues with professional learning, looking at both preservice preparation and in-service professional development. To set the stage for these discussions, Tricia Shelton (National Science Teaching Association) presented details about a recent educator survey on standards implementation.

SETTING THE STAGE: NSTA SURVEY

The National Science Teaching Association (NSTA) is the largest organization in the world committed to promoting excellence and innovation in science teaching and learning for all, said Shelton. The panelists and the discussion at this Summit, she said, have surfaced how our commitment to the *Framework* and the NGSS has stayed strong for the past decade, and at the same time highlighted that our understanding of how we can enact that vision has evolved. NSTA has mirrored this evolution, recently developing a new digital engagement strategy and rethinking how to support the work of educators and students. NSTA has shifted its approach to the *Framework* and the NGSS to a "learning first" approach, said Shelton, which centers on providing teachers with "what they articulate that they need at the time that they need it."

One of the ways that NSTA keeps its "fingers on the pulse" of what is going on across the nation is by asking educators to share their voices through surveys, as well as anecdotal evidence collected at conferences and focus groups. Shelton shared the results of a recent survey on science standards implementation. The survey focused on three main question areas:

- What are the main challenges in implementing science standards in ways that connect science to students and their home communities?
- What are important messages to send to leaders?
- What are important features of excellent science instruction?

There were 197 survey respondents, with representation from pre–K to college. Educators working in elementary, middle, and high schools identified time as one of the biggest challenges to implementation of standards, said Shelton. Following closely behind time were resources and materials, and teachers in the higher grades identified an additional challenge of the instructional shifts necessary to implement standards well. With states all over the country enacting new science standards at different times, Shelton said that there has been a tension between teaching the standards in high school, while also honoring the fact that many students in K–8 classrooms were not enacting the new standards.

The second question of the survey identified important messages for leaders. These included, said Shelton, that science is important and be a priority; implementation of the standards will require professional learning, resources, support, time, and funding; and attention be paid to alignment and coherence, assessments, and the emphasis on 3-D learning. Finally, said Shelton, survey respondents identified important features of excellent instruction. They described it as hands-on or inquiry based, relevant to the local community and students' lives, phenomenon-based, and student-centered, taught by knowledgeable teachers who emphasize collaboration.

PRESERVICE PREPARATION

Victor Sampson (University of Texas at Austin) moderated this session of the Summit by asking questions of the four panelists:

- Melissa Braaten: assistant professor of STEM education and teacher education at University of Colorado, Boulder; former science teacher; focuses on preparing justice-oriented teachers to work in diverse communities
- Lizette Burks: assistant professor of education leadership at University of Houston-Downtown; served as state science supervisor in Kansas; focuses on improving educational opportunities for youth in historically disadvantaged communities
- Todd Campbell: Department Head of Curriculum Construction and professor of science education at University of Connecticut; focuses on cultivating equitable representations of STEM activity
- Thomas Philip: professor and faculty director of teacher education at University of California, Berkeley; focuses on how teachers make sense of power and hierarchy in the classroom, schools, and society

Undergraduate and Graduate Programs

> *What has your teacher education program done, or is currently in the process of doing, to help preservice science teachers learn to create and facilitate rigorous and equitable learning experiences for students in a way that is aligned with the recommendations found in the Framework?*

University of Colorado, Boulder

The undergraduate elementary program at University of Colorado, Boulder, said Braaten, prepares teachers to teach grades K–6, and also prepares them to have an endorsement to work in solidarity with communities that are culturally and linguistically diverse. This program begins with a course offered freshman year that gives students an opportunity to "dip their toes" into thinking about what it means to teach science and math in elementary settings for justice-oriented purposes. In this class, said Braaten, students work closely with families and community organizations on interest-driven STEM experiences. For example, during the early days of the pandemic, students worked with a foster network organization to develop ideas about doing science at home. The students designed experiences for foster families and shared back and forth with the families about their experiences. In students' senior year, they work with mentor teachers and teacher activists who are interested in making principled adaptations to instructional materials. In this experience, said Braaten, students and teachers work to redesign materials to support bilingualism, to push back against de facto English-only policies, and to try to orient science toward equity and justice wherever possible. For example, a unit about butterfly life cycles is common in elementary settings. The students reoriented this unit to look at pollination in the local ecosystem and to consider how climate change is disrupting pollination. Making these changes "requires a lot of advocacy and agency on the part of our preservice teachers," said Braaten.

University of Connecticut

The University of Connecticut is a predominantly white institution, said Campbell, which has resulted in "structures that limit who participates and who becomes teachers." The university is evaluating its program to consider how it could be more inclusive and how to push back against the systemic racism that is built in. For example, he said, which students could commit to a student teacher semester, and which students would find it challenging? As part of these efforts, there is a student-led organization that brings people to campus to talk about anti-racist practices and to push the faculty to change and grow. Campbell shared details about the university's methods class, which focuses on thinking about "who we are and how that shapes what we do, what we think, what we value, and what we prioritize." The students reflect on their own identities and consider how their identities might operate when connecting and working with the community. Much of the class time is spent doing rehearsals, said Campbell, thinking about moment-to-moment interactions with students. During these rehearsals, the class uses high-quality curriculum materials and discusses issues of equity and expanding the concept of science. Toward the end of the semester, students develop a relevant and justice-focused curriculum.

University of Arkansas

Burks worked to develop a new two-year graduate program at the University of Arkansas that focused on supporting teacher quality in underserved school districts. The program was funded with grant money and was tuition-free; many of the teachers in the program were alternatively certified or had traveled nontraditional paths into education. The courses developed for the program used traditional science methods knowledge, because Burks heard from many early career educators that they were missing some of this content. With limited time to prepare educators, Burks said it was useful to use 3-D science classroom assessments as a lever to create equitable learning experiences aligned to the *Framework*.

University of California, Berkeley

Philip presented from his perspective as the faculty director of the teacher education program at University of California, Berkeley; specifically, he explored the conditions and contexts within the program that allow for rigorous and equitable learning environments for students. Another way of looking at this, he said, is to ask, "How do we create programmatic systems where both teacher educators and preservice teachers can thrive as teachers and learners?" Because the Berkeley program is new, there was an opportunity to develop it in a systematic and thoughtful way, said Philip. There were two components to this, he said. First, was ensuring that the pieces of the program fit together so that the courses complement each other and are integrated with field experiences. Second, was a "huge cultural shift" of the role of faculty instructors, supervisors, and cooperating teachers. It is critical to recognize the significance of what educators bring to teacher education as individuals, he said, along with the university and credientialing demands. This work has been done through examining how mundane organizational activities are conducted, and how these decisions either further the vision or do not. For example, said Philip, it is important to look at how programs are designed, when and how meetings are run, and where and how colleagues have opportunities to collaborate. Although these "seemingly unremarkable" activities are commonplace in teacher education programs, there is a need to "elevate the ordinary" to see how programs support the learning of both teacher educators and teachers. Philip said that preparing new teachers to create and facilitate rigorous and equitable learning experiences for students has entailed an incredible amount of invisible, inward-facing, and internal work that supports all constituents of the program to see each other's work through a programmatic lens.

Challenges

Time

> *How do you find time in undergraduate programs to develop the skills needed and bring groups together to collaborate?*

Braaten said she has 14 Fridays to prepare people to enter their career as an elementary school teacher, so she spends a large amount of time outside of class setting the stage to make the most of those 14 Fridays. Braaten said that she tries not to assign too much work to be done outside of class, because preservice teachers are usually teaching full time while taking their senior year of coursework. By spending time conversing with teacher activists and organizations outside of class, these collaborators can "hit the ground running" to support the preservice teachers during class time. Burks added that she seeks to leverage high-quality, equity-focused resources, networks, and supports to maximize the short amount of time she has to support teachers.

Alignment

> *How can teacher preparation programs contend with the misalignment sometimes observed between teacher preparation coursework and the experiences that preservice teachers have in local schools during their field experiences?*

Sampson asked panelists to comment on how they have navigated this misalignment in their programs. Campbell replied that he tries to focus on keeping "the most important thing the most important thing." He wants to engage people deeply in science, while at the same time testing what science is. This includes, he said, unpacking the NGSS to see how it fits and connects with the work of inclusion and equity. The starting point is not the standards; rather, the starting point is "figuring out what we're trying to accomplish." Burks said that in Arkansas, many school district administrators navigate the tension of meeting expectations for state assessments that were often not fully aligned to the science content standards. This tension was discussed early in the relationship-building process with partners, she said, and partner school districts were chosen based on whether they could help the goals of both the program and the community. In addition, the program partnered with other organizations—such as the Arkansas Department of Education—to support the alignment of efforts across the state. Educators in the program were provided stipends to join state and national science learning communities (e.g., NSTA), which increased network support for educators. Burks said that moving beyond the university silo to work with people and existing efforts at the state, district, and building levels was a critical piece of the program.

Campbell agreed that alignment is a challenge and said that preservice teachers are asked to traverse the two different worlds of the university and the classroom. One way to mitigate this tension, said Campbell, is to partner with schools and to consider them as part of a unified system. University of Connecticut has a mentor teacher collaborative made up of teachers who have hosted preservice teachers. The objective of the group is to engage in professional learning but at the same time to consider how professional learning can benefit preservice teachers. Campbell said that collaborating and sharing resources among teacher education programs is useful but that the work that happens in local communities is "unique and cultured." There is a need to recognize the "pluriverse" in which educators are working hard and collaborating but without the expectation of finding one way of doing things.

Philip said that although it is true that there are disjunctures between the university and the field, he is concerned that focusing on these may "inadvertently perpetuate some problematic stances toward teaching." Focusing on misalignment may encourage new teachers to judge and dismiss a veteran teacher's practices rather than learning to ask questions and to have deliberate dialogue about the assumptions and consequences of different practices. Although we do not want preservice teachers to think that all practices are equally consequential, we do want them to think about "the ethics of practice, who benefits, who is marginalized, and under what conditions" with particular practices. Apparent misalignments can be used as an opportunity for preservice teachers to learn how to engage in dialogue about their practice, and as an opportunity for beneficial institutional transformation across universities and partner schools.

Braaten agreed with Philip and said that although preservice teachers report dissonance between the university and the classroom, she does not see this as a problem. Rather, she said, it reflects the fact that there are always differences between settings, and it is a chance to learn and talk together with partners. Viewing it in this way frames partners as people to build with and work with rather than people that "you're trying to judge or compete with." At University of Colorado, Boulder, classes offer opportunities to consider how preservice teachers can navigate these tensions and team up with mentor teachers to advocate for more robust science education. Braaten noted that they do this work not just for science-related issues but also for navigating oppressive practices in the classroom (e.g., ableist or heteronormative practices). Preservice teachers are encouraged and supported in learning how to advocate and exercise agency in their teaching, said Braaten.

TEACHER PROFESSIONAL DEVELOPMENT

Shelton introduced this session of the Summit by describing three critical aspects of her own journey of personal-professional learning. Shelton was a secondary science teacher in Kentucky, a state that was an early adopter of the NGSS. Her district, she said, took a sustained professional learning approach that gave her and others the space to learn and the space to try new things within the classroom. Shelton said that this gave her the confidence to partner with her students in enacting the *Framework*. Second, many partner organizations throughout Kentucky supported teachers in implementation efforts by creating communities of practice. Within these communities, there were opportunities to dialogue with other teachers throughout the state who were engaged in the same work, and to interact with researchers and leaders who were leading implementation efforts at the state, regional, and district levels. The third critical aspect, said Shelton, is that the leadership in Kentucky "put teachers at the table from day one." Leaders in the state believed that teachers are equipped to co-lead educational change; Shelton said that this was critical to her success in the classroom as well as in her professional development that led her to her work at NSTA. Shelton introduced the panel, which was composed of five individuals with varied experience, expertise, and perspective in the professional learning space.

- Jody Bintz: associate director at BSCS Science Learning; focuses on strategic partnerships and professional learning
- K. Renae Pullen: elementary science specialist for Caddo Parish Public Schools; supports teachers and school leaders
- Breigh Rhodes: director of math, science, and STEM at the Louisiana Department of Education
- Stacey van der Veen: Leadership in Science, LLC
- Julie Yu: senior scientist at Exploratorium

Vision of Implementation

What are some of the different trends observed with respect to the implementation of the vision of the Framework?

Standards implementation is outcome-oriented, said Bintz, with the goal of producing "a citizenry ready, willing, and able to attend to 21st century challenges." BSCS considers the broad and effective use of high-quality instructional materials, supported by curriculum-based professional learning, as an important system component to ensure equity and access. High-quality instructional materials are an important lever because they offer a "ubiquitous presence" for students and teachers in the classroom. Bintz said that the *Framework* and the NGSS have resulted in greater availability of these materials and thus better opportunities for students and teachers. Curriculum-based professional learning is essential for preparing teachers to use these materials, she said, and strong leadership is critical for supporting teachers in their development.

Caddo Parish Public Schools, said Pullen, has a vision of science learning in which students investigate, evaluate, and reason scientifically; apply their content knowledge to real-world phenomena; and think creatively and make connections. To implement this vision, teachers need to understand the 3-D standards and have access to rich phenomena-based curricula. Teachers who have these resources—and who have the time and space to use them—are making the instructional shifts necessary to achieve the vision, said Pullen. However, teachers who do not yet have curricula available "struggle a little bit" to make the instructional shifts. Pullen said that school leaders are often left out of professional learning and that this disconnect can make it difficult for teachers to enact the vision of the *Framework*.

At the Louisiana Department of Education, said Rhodes, the vision of implementation centers on the belief that selecting and faithfully implementing high-quality curricula and materials is one of things that can have the biggest impacts on student learning. Implementation requires ongoing professional development that is aligned to the *Framework*, as well as to Louisiana's aligned assessments. Rhodes said that the core strategies of the department focus on those three elements: high-quality materials, professional development, and assessments. Currently, between 70 and 82 percent of Louisiana's systems are reporting adoption of high-quality materials and ongoing professional development. However, she said, "adoption and implementation are not the same thing." Implementation means that all students are participating in meaningful 3-D science, and that all teachers are fully prepared to deliver high-quality instruction every day. In addition, implementation means that there are systems of support in place, teachers have the materials they need, and the master schedule allows adequate time for teaching and planning. In the process of implementation, said Rhodes, there are "beautiful things" happening. For example, teachers are sharing vulnerabilities about how to navigate the "scary unknown" of student-centered, phenomena-based teaching and learning. Teachers are persevering through these challenges, she said, which means that they see the value that implementation holds for their students.

When implementation is fully realized, said van der Veen, teachers engage students in investigations of phenomena, these investigations are driven by 3-D tasks, and this work is done with the full support of administrators and school systems. van der Veen described the three areas of her work: conducting workshops for teachers and administrators that focus on the vision behind the *Framework*; observing the process of implementing this vision in the classroom; and working with leaders to support teachers in this work. van der Veen said that teachers who embrace even part of the vision feel "empowered and excited" by it. One teacher, she said, reported that she felt like a new teacher again, "in a good way." This excitement of learning, engaging, and pushing oneself "feeds teachers" and makes them want more. However, said van der Veen, the system largely doesn't support this work. She said that teachers often leave the workshop excited to implement 3-D learning, but their plans get derailed by the realities of day-to-day teaching in their school.

The Exploratorium, said Yu, was created to provide opportunities for people to engage with science rather than simply receive science. She said that the philosophy in their teacher professional learning programs is no different—teachers deserve sustained professional learning that engages them in learning experiences to help them understand how they are being asked to teach. Part of the excitement of science class is seeing students figure things out, said Yu, and providing opportunities for learning experiences where teachers can figure things out is an important step in making that happen in the classroom.

Status of Implementation

What do we know about the status of implementation of the vision behind the Framework?

The status of implementation is "wildly uneven," said van der Veen. There are teachers who come to workshops with only a passing understanding of the NGSS, and there are other teachers who have been "digging deeply" into this work since the *Framework* was published. Generally, said van der Veen, teachers struggle to translate what they have learned in professional development into classroom practice. One reason for this is the "dailiness" of school—that is, the day-to-day pressures and responsibilities of teachers. Another reason for this struggle is that trying new things can feel unsafe to teachers; administrators may not understand the reason for change or trust teachers to do their work. Teachers are also perfectionists, said van der Veen. They hold themselves to a high standard and are hesitant to implement something with their students unless it is "neatly tied in a bow." van der Veen said that she urges teachers not to let the perfect be the enemy of the good. In her work, van der Veen observes how teachers bring lessons from workshops back into the classroom. She said that the teachers who successfully implement new practices tend to plan collaboratively with colleagues and to engage in deep discourse around practice. van der Veen added that during the past year and a half of the COVID-19 pandemic, she has observed that teachers who were already engaged in NGSS-aligned instruction found the transition to hybrid or remote learning much easier because students were already at the center of the investigations. These teachers and students were already applying scientific inquiries to real-world phenomena—from students' backyards to kitchens—and thus were more readily able to pivot out of the classroom.

Rhodes reported that there is growing buy-in across Louisiana, and she said that there are two indicators of this trend. First, educators are demanding more in terms of professional development and materials. She noted that when the NGSS were first released, there was a lot of hesitation; educators wanted to continue using their own lessons and didn't want to be told what to do. However, now they are eager to participate in trainings and use new materials to align their teaching and learning with the vision of the *Framework* and the NGSS. Second, Rhodes said that during the pandemic, she observed that many educators strived to continue to implement high-quality science education. For example, she said, one teacher reached out to her and said he was unwilling to "settle for some flashy computer program." He and other teachers demanded more for their students and worked to adapt and share materials so that they could be used in virtual or hybrid settings. Rhodes said that these types of materials can now be found online for teachers across the country because educators were willing to do the difficult work to give their students the education they deserve.

The status of implementation varies widely across California, said Yu. However, regardless of where teachers are in the process, they are "hungry for professional learning." Professional development requires time, she said, and this time should be compensated. In addition, quality professional development recognizes and addresses the different needs of teachers, whether those are related to grade level, local context, or personal identities. Yu compared the process of implementation to running a marathon. "Around mile 20 you might hit a wall," she said, and noted that the pandemic put up a "pretty serious wall" during efforts to implement the *Framework*. However, she said, "this is not the time to back off the gas pedal." Instead, it is time to "hydrate and add calories" and push forward toward implementation of the *Framework*.

Challenges to Implementation

> *What are some of the obstacles to implementation and how can they be addressed?*

The obstacles in the way of implementation, said Pullen, are the usual suspects: policies, lack of support, and decision makers. Existing policies do not support science education, and in some cases actively oppose it. There is little time allotted for science, particularly now with the anxiety of learning loss, she said. Some policies unintentionally exacerbate inequalities for students who are already historically excluded from science learning. There is little funding and time for professional development or the curriculum resources to support educators. One "surprising" policy barrier, said Pullen, is that due to high student-teacher ratios, there is sometimes no physical space for investigations and designs to take place. The lack of support can be seen in a lack of time for teachers to collaborate and plan with each other and a lack of quality and engaging curricula. Pullen noted that even when curricula are free, implementing them in the classroom has costs in terms of professional learning and time for teachers. Decision makers can serve as barriers to implementation because they often do not come from a science background, which means they don't understand the vision or the need for teaching science differently. The solution to all these barriers, said Pullen, is to start teaching science early to all young learners, regardless of the zip code of their school. To do this, teachers need to be supported as they improve their practices, leaders need to be supported in order to support teachers, and funding and policies need to be aligned with these goals.

Bintz agreed that zip code shouldn't limit the science learning opportunities for students and added that it also shouldn't impact the professional learning opportunities for teachers. High-quality, curriculum-based professional learning is expensive and takes a lot of time, energy, and commitment, she said. As teachers develop a vision for a *Framework*-based approach to teaching and learning, leaders need to be encouraged and supported in getting on board and providing the resources needed to achieve the vision.

van der Veen identified four barriers to implementation that she has observed in her work. First, some districts substitute instructional materials for curriculum. Teachers get an "unwieldy" kit with hundreds of pages, and administrators encourage them to use it. Second, van der Veen agreed with Bintz and Pullen's statements about administrators and leaders being a barrier to implementation. To overcome this barrier, it is critical to engage administrators meaningfully and purposefully in workshops "elbow-to-elbow" with teachers. van der Veen noted that she won't work with a district unless it commits to sending administrators and teachers together, because otherwise it is "unfair to the administrators and it is unfair to the teachers." Administrators' discomfort and unfamiliarity is a "huge obstacle" to implementation, she said, but "it is not that hard to chip away at it." Third, there is a lack of support for teachers to work together and learn from each other. This work is too big and too difficult to accomplish alone, and teachers need time to think together. She said that some teachers from the same school have never had the opportunity to sit down and engage in deep discourse around practice until they attended a workshop together. A final obstacle at this moment, said van der Veen, is a critical lack of substitute teachers, at least within New Jersey; without substitutes, teachers cannot participate in many professional learning opportunities.

The Role of Partnerships in Implementation

What role have partnerships played in local and state implementation efforts?

Yu offered two examples of partnerships from her work in California. At an organizational level, she said, the Exploratorium is part of a coalition of stakeholders that includes county offices of education, districts, professional associations, academic researchers, informal organizations, and policy makers. The Exploratorium recently hosted a convening of coalition members to create coherence and identify priorities for science education so that the "same narrative" is reinforced across the state. Yu noted that as an informal science organization, the Exploratorium has a unique opportunity to serve as the hub for the broader science education community. She also noted that the Exploratorium has direct connections with scientists, teachers, researchers, districts, and families, and said that they can leverage these relationships in order to engage and connect the community. The second example that Yu gave was a statewide network of teacher-leaders and professional learning providers who support teachers in their local context. Members of the network, which was organized specifically around NGSS implementation, have access to ongoing workshops, a listserv, and communities of practice that each focus on a topic (e.g., social justice). Yu said that the network leverages the on-the-ground knowledge of teachers who are in both formal and informal leadership roles and activates people in these roles to be a part of implementation. "We celebrate their work, and we compensate them for their time," said Yu.

Although high-quality materials and professional learning are essential to implementation, said Rhodes, "we are always going to fall short" without partnerships. The Louisiana Department of Education thinks about partnerships in two ways, she said. First, the department can serve as a matchmaker to connect people with opportunities and resources, and to facilitate relationships. Second, the department is exploring ways to be a better partner to individuals and organizations outside the formal space, such as afterschool program coordinators. Bintz agreed that the effort of implementation "requires a village" and that partnerships are key. It is critical not only to develop relationships with like-minded partners but also to communicate and partner with those with diverse perspectives. There will always be challenges involved in the effort to implement the vision of the NGSS and the *Framework*, she said, and it will take strong partnership relationships to stay the course, overcome the challenges, and bring the best possible learning opportunities to teachers and students.

DISCUSSION

> *What should the field be doing to better support new and experienced teachers in their implementation efforts in a way that is coherent, equitable, and inclusive?*

In this session, speakers from both the preservice preparation and the professional development panels answered the question posed by Sampson.

Supporting Teachers

Yu began with a simple axiom: Practice what you preach. She explained that people who provide or facilitate professional learning need to ensure that the experience teachers have in professional learning "matches and maps" to what they are being asked to do in the classroom. For example, if teachers are being asked to use equitable science teaching practices, they need to experience and feel this in their own professional learning. Yu said that one component of equitable science teaching is for all students to have science teachers that represent the ethnic diversity of their communities. Because there are fewer teachers of color in science and they have lower rates of retention, Yu and her organization have expanded their work to sustain and support teachers of color through exploring their identities, leveraging personal experiences, and reshaping the system around them to gain ownership and agency. Although none of this is explicitly in the standards, Yu said it is essential to implementing the standards equitably. The bottom line, she said, is that "the way you are working with teachers as learners needs to reflect how you want teachers to work with students as learners." Burks agreed with Yu's call for equitable science learning and teaching and said that it would be enormously valuable to have explicit standards for diversity, equity, and inclusion in science education.

Pullen agreed with Yu that all science teachers deserve access to sustainable, ongoing, equitable professional learning opportunities; she added that these opportunities be part of an intentional professional learning development plan that progresses over time. Pullen said that implementation and the associated professional learning are not linear processes. Although districts may have detailed plans for implementing curricula, teachers may enter the process at different points and they need to be supported and engaged in getting caught up. She emphasized that administrators and leaders need to be part of this learning as well so that they can better understand the conceptual shifts in science and support teachers in their efforts to improve science teaching and learning. Bintz added that another critical element is helping teachers and administrators see the vision of *Framework*-aligned teaching and learning. Video is useful for showing people what this looks like in the classroom, whether it is culturally responsive teaching, phenomena-based learning, or 3-D teaching and learning. When teachers have high-quality instructional materials and they know how to use them and are able to make decisions moment-to-moment, said Bintz, they are prepared to help students be ready to attend to 21st century challenges.

"It is really important that we help teachers connect back to why they teach science," said van der Veen. Teachers have many reasons—they love science, they want students to meaningfully engage in their community, and they want students to understand that there is power in learning from mistakes. However, these reasons can "fall apart" when trying to implement standards and to deal with day-to-day challenges. van der Veen urged participants to help teachers stay centered on their reasons for teaching science and to connect these reasons to the vision behind the *Framework*. "Connecting the why to the how" is something that can be explicitly done, she said. In addition, we need to recognize that the shifts that are required of teachers to engage in *Framework*-aligned instruction are "huge, significant shifts." They are being asked to learn and teach in ways that they have not experienced, and in ways that are very different from what they have learned and practiced. van der Veen repeated Yu's exhortation for teachers to be given educational opportunities that are like what we are asking them to design for their students.

Resources

Braaten sketched her vision of what she would like to be able to do in an ideal world. Currently, she works with six districts across Colorado, and has to tap into philanthropy and grant funding to do work that "should be core work infrastructure" by the school district and state. For example, Braaten said she would love to conduct intergenerational science professional development and would want to compensate participants for their time; however, if she has to "scramble for funding," it is not sustainable. Another disconnect between the current situation and Braaten's vision has to do with the sustainability and continuity of professional learning. Braaten said that she works with districts that have a teacher turnover rate so high that the entire workforce turns over about every three years. In an ideal world, teachers would be engaged in long-term professional learning that builds on itself, but this is not possible with such high turnover. Braaten said that moving from the current scenario to her vision "boils down" to committing resources toward the core work of teaching and learning.

Philip agreed that resources are a big challenge, noting that the cost of earning a credential at the university is continuing to increase, and private foundations and venture philanthropists are exerting their financial resources to shape the direction of teacher education. In light of this, it is more important than ever to deeply engage with the public about the purpose of public education and teacher education, and about collective participation in our systems. "We cannot genuinely move toward more equitable and rigorous learning" without this kind of intentional dialogue. Braaten added that there is a need to ensure that the relationship between student teachers and teacher mentors is mutually beneficial. In Colorado, student teachers can now be paid for their work; however, the issue of who pays them has not been settled. Teacher mentors also need compensation for their work, whether in the form of money, continuing credit, or whatever teachers find valuable in their own practice, said Braaten.

Materials

Many speakers, said Sampson, have noted that there is an increasing number of high-quality curricular materials available to support teachers with instructional approaches that are aligned with the *Framework* and the NGSS. Sampson asked speakers to comment on how teacher education programs are preparing teachers to use these materials. Braaten responded that in Colorado, each district they work with has adopted different materials.

In the teacher education program at the University of Colorado, Boulder, they give candidates opportunities to analyze open access materials, using a variety of *Framework* tools. In addition, candidates evaluate materials based on issues such as equity or students who are English language learners. Braaten said that they encourage candidates to become familiar with the curricular materials that are available, and to consider them as being "just the starting point" for curriculum building. She stressed that materials are just one tool out of many tools that teachers draw upon to build the pedagogies used in their classrooms. Bintz agreed with this assessment and compared teaching to gardening. She explained that just as a gardener has to make decisions about what to pull out of the ground, what to leave, and what to plant, teachers have to make decisions about how and whether to use existing materials, and how to adapt and adjust based on the context in which they are teaching.

Equity

The word "equity" can bring people together but can also act to obscure different fundamental assumptions about the world, said Philip. For example, one notion of equity might lead us toward the goal of getting more children involved in science. Another notion of equity, however, is based on the idea that science itself is integral and co-constitutive of some of the inequities and injustices that exist. This notion would point toward a goal of "changing science as we know it." When engaged in discourses around equity, Philip said, it is critical that we identify the underlying assumptions and consequences of different notions of equity. Philip put forth three stances that he said could be helpful when engaging in equitable implementation. First, ensure that collaborations and partnerships center mutual learning, mutual benefit, and mutual transformation. Second, enter collaborations and partnerships with humility and attention to the dynamics of power. Third, start from the premise that implementation is an ongoing, iterative process, and that there is a need "to constantly examine how our work might be reproducing or challenging existing inequities." Furthermore, Philip said that there is a need to consider the hierarchies that exist within teacher education itself—who does the bulk of the work, who gets to write about it, who gets to publish on it, and what is considered worthy of scholarly attention?

Role of Outside Champions

Rhodes encouraged participants to engage with partners and leaders beyond the traditional science education community. For example, a principal without a science background could be a champion for implementation if he or she appreciates the vision of the *Framework* and the NGSS. These types of champions can use their roles to support teachers, give them time and space, and help eliminate obstacles. There are also potential champions that can contribute to professional development, said Rhodes. For example, groups such as the Center for Black Educators can contribute unique expertise and help make professional learning more relevant and useful for educators.

Collaboration

This Summit, said Campbell, has made it clear that there is a strong collective community around science education that together is "accomplishing great things." It is critical to continue to make connections with other individuals and to share resources, he said, and he emphasized that we should not strive to implement identical programs across the country but rather to create momentum around the tools and thinking that other people have developed. For example, said Campbell, districts in Connecticut are working together to implement *Framework*-aligned science education and they are basing their work on four essential features of the NGSS. van der Veen agreed that collaboration among teachers and others is essential for implementation, and she said that teachers need to be taught the norms of collaboration; need time, space, and support to collaborate; and need "fading scaffolds of facilitation" so that collaborative conversations are rich and focused on practice. Most importantly, she said, we need to "recognize how hard this work is," and give teachers the time and space to learn and grow together.

7

Curriculum and Instructional Materials

Public opinion of the NGSS is high, said Sam Shaw (EdReports.org). A study published by the American Educational Research Association found that the NGSS is popular with educators and the feelings of positivity increase year after year (EdReports, 2021). However, he said, not all materials in the field are aligned with the vision of the *Framework*. For the innovations in the *Framework* and the NGSS to take hold, teachers need high-quality instructional materials (HQIM) that help students solve problems using ideas and practices rather than merely teaching an isolated topic (EdReports, 2021). In addition, said Shaw, it is critical that materials attend to student diversity and equity, while at the same time support teacher professional learning (Campbell and Lee, 2021).

Shaw shared data about the materials that are currently available and in use. The majority of materials used in science classrooms are commercially published textbooks, which include supplementary materials such as worksheets and laboratory handouts. Classrooms may also use materials that are developed by states, counties, districts, and dioceses; resources from free or subscription-based websites; commercially published kits and online courses (see Table 7-1).

A survey of educators found that 20 percent of science teachers regularly use materials that pre-date the NGSS, and 42 percent of science teachers regularly use materials that they created themselves. More than half of teachers reported that they had never participated in workshops, trainings, or coaching that was focused on use of science materials, although 65 percent said that they did engage in collaborative learning with other teachers around materials (EdReports, 2021).

TABLE 7-1 Science Classes for Which Various Types of Instructional Resources Are Designated, by Grade Range

	Percent of Classes		
	Elementary	Middle	High
Commercially published textbooks (printed or electronic), including the supplementary materials (e.g., worksheets, laboratory handouts) that accompany the textbooks	67 (2.9)	87 (1.8)	95 (0.9)
State, county, district, or diocese-developed units or lessons	43 (2.2)	32 (2.3)	27 (1.7)
Lessons or resources from websites that are free (e.g., Khan Academy, PhET)	20 (1.9)	26 (2.2)	25 (2.0)
Commercially published kits/modules (printed or electronic)	51 (2.7)	36 (3.1)	22 (2.0)
Lessons or resources from websites that have a subscription fee or per lesson cost (e.g., BrainPOP, Discovery Ed, Teachers Pay Teachers)	39 (2.7)	39 (2.8)	16 (1.5)
Online units or courses that students work through at their own pace (e.g., i-Ready, Edgenuity)	9 (1.2)	15 (2.0)	11 (1.8)

NOTE: Includes only those teachers who indicated that their randomly selected science class had an instructional material designated by the state, district, or diocese.
SOURCE: Banilower et al. (2018).

Past work has informed this session of the workshop, said Shaw. For example, at a previous National Academies workshop, *Design, Selection, and Implementation of Instructional Materials for the Next Generation Science Standards* (NASEM, 2018), speakers discussed the next steps for ensuring that materials aligned with the NGSS were developed and made available to educators. These next steps, said Shaw, included improving the review process with a broad coalition of stakeholders, and increasing interconnection among supply, demand, and implementation. More recently, a special issue of the *Journal of Science Teacher Education* (Volume 32, Issue 7) featured commentary and research on topics including project-based learning, large-scale transformation, and the role of professional learning. Specific programs were highlighted for the progress they have made in policies, practices, and programs.

With this and other previous work in mind, this session of the workshop was designed to talk about the current state of curriculum and instructional materials implementation and opportunities moving forward, as well as to identify tools and resources needed to advance a more just, equitable, and inclusive learning experience. Shaw moderated the session by asking questions of the six panelists:

- Philip Bell, University of Washington
- Cory Epler, Nebraska Department of Education
- Dora Kastel, New Visions for Public Schools
- Spencer Martin, Kansas City Public Schools
- Carol O'Donnell, Smithsonian Science Education Center
- Jamie Rumage, Oregon Department of Education

THE ROLE OF HIGH-QUALITY INSTRUCTIONAL MATERIALS

> *What is the single most important thing that instructional materials can bring to support quality science learning for each and every child?*

O'Donnell said that from the perspective of curriculum developers, she believes that materials should not only respond to the needs of schools (i.e., be aligned with the standards) but also provide point of view support for teachers to respond to students' current contexts. That is, she explained, they be "nimble, adaptable to local contexts, responsive to cultural needs, and place based." Importantly, equity should be at the forefront in the creation of materials, said O'Donnell. Bell said that a broadly developed curriculum can provide a platform for teachers and students to make science learning relevant to their lives. "The cultural lives of learners have not been deeply centered in instructional experience" as they need to be, he said, and HQIM can serve to help center learners and provide openings for the assets that learners bring to the table. Rumage added that it is critical to consider "who is and who is not written into our instructional materials" and "whose contributions, whose histories, whose ways of knowing" are being privileged. She said that this goes beyond diverse pictorial representation and into whether materials intentionally create space to study localized and relevant phenomena, or problems that foster students' interests, identity, culture, and agency. "Every student wants to be seen and valued," she said, "and if that student can't see themselves, their families, or their communities in the materials they often feel like they don't belong."

Several speakers noted the importance of teacher support and training in the use of HQIM. Epler said that HQIM are enormously important, but there are multiple other pieces that are necessary for their implementation, including teacher professional learning. Martin agreed with this perspective and said that while quality materials are necessary to realize the vision of the NGSS, they are not sufficient without teacher development, teacher support, and teacher capacity building. He added that teachers need time to practice their craft, and administrators need to acknowledge and address this need. "Time is something that all the teachers we work with always say we don't have enough of," said Kastel. Teachers are expected to become experts on multiple topics, she said, including virtual and hybrid teaching, culturally responsive education, various models and frameworks, and designing classroom materials. This is "too much," said Kastel; providing high-quality materials, along with professional learning, can free teachers up to focus on their students.

TRADEOFFS BETWEEN GOALS

Reflecting on the vision for science education present in the Framework, what decisions are made in NGSS design that promote high outcomes for all students and center the idea that all students have opportunities to learn? What tradeoffs are inherent in designing instruction?

Local vs. Global Phenomena

When designing curriculum, said Kastel, "anchor phenomena" are used to give students an entry point into the subject matter. The challenge, she said, is determining whether these phenomena be locally relevant or globally relevant. Furthermore, "what does local mean" in a place like New York, where students may have different experiences and perspectives in the Bronx versus Manhattan versus Brooklyn? To address this challenge, said Kastel, students begin the unit with a "related phenomena routine" where they have an opportunity to make connections with the anchor phenomena to make it relevant to them.

Bell said that this issue with anchor phenomena is something that he and his colleagues "think about pretty deeply and carefully," and that the field is building collective capacity to address the challenge. He offered a metaphor of materials being like the base recipe for a main dish. The recipe encapsulates the "educationally nutritious and tasty" parts, but it is intended to be modified and adapted based on local expertise, ingredients, and context, and perhaps to be supplemented with other "tasty dishes." However, when considering anchor phenomena, it is critical to think about whose interests are being served by the selection of phenomena. If the interests and perceptions of students who have been historically disenfranchised are different than the interests and perceptions of students who have historically been better served, Bell said, "we should be choosing the phenomena for the students that have been historically disenfranchised." Bell gave an example of this type of decision making. A unit that was developed for middle schoolers to study light included justice-centered dimensions of light, such as medical imaging devices and facial recognition devices that have racial bias that would impact students and community members. Bell said that this type of approach allows students to critically engage in an analysis of injustice, and to explore how tools could be designed that are more fair and just. These types of justice-centered phenomena are a growing focus, he said, and he is excited to see how the field centers this and other dimensions of learning in relation to science and engineering.

The use of localized phenomena, said Rumage, can help students see concepts as relevant to their everyday lives, particularly students who may not see themselves as scientists. However, it is challenging for material developers to deeply understand the regional and localized contexts, so there is flexibility for educators to adjust or manipulate the materials based on their immediate localized learning needs. Rumage shared an example of a school in Oregon that was using instructional materials that were not reflective of their student population, nor coherent across multiple years and subjects. The students who were particularly impacted by this situation, she said, were those with disabilities and students of color. The school responded by developing an intentional three-year high school course sequence that utilizes open-license materials that are built for educators by educators within the localized context. This provided opportunities, said Rumage, for hyperlocalized materials, for professional learning, and for integrated curriculum. Although courses and materials "won't undo the deeply historic and systematic oppression our students experience," she said, it is an example of how a school can leverage funds to create effective learning opportunities for students.

Alignment vs. Usability

There is a tradeoff, said Kastel, between making materials that meet every criterion for alignment with the NGSS and making materials that are usable and accessible for teachers. She said that when trying to "check off every box," materials end up being "incredibly dense and incredibly bulky." These types of materials can be a barrier, particularly for novice teachers, teachers who are new to the NGSS, and teachers who don't have access to professional learning to support using materials. When we are asking teachers to shift roles from instructor to facilitator, she said, it is critical that they have materials and support to help them in this shift. Relatedly, there is a tension for teachers between fidelity to the materials versus adapting them to their particular needs and context. For example, materials that were created before 2020 were designed to build on grade standards, but due to the pandemic, many students may not be at these levels. It is essential that teachers have ways to modify materials to be useful for their students. The bottom line, said Kastel, is that professional learning and coaching are essential to support the decision making and adapting that teachers need to do, and we cannot "truly be successful at scale without it."

Martin agreed that the development of materials to meet all the criteria can sometimes result in a "500-page unit guide that no one is ever going to read." In his first few years as an instructional coach, he said, he made the mistake of simply handing teachers materials and resources rather than "rolling up [his] sleeves" and working with teachers to figure out how to actually use them in the classroom. The tension between alignment and usability is very real; it is difficult to develop a resource that can scaffold and support teachers, while still being doable for teachers with little planning time. It is important to design resources with the NGSS goals in mind, yet also allow for the autonomy and professional experience of teachers. If this tension is not acknowledged, the standards will "live up in the ivory tower" rather than be implemented in classrooms. Part of the challenge, said Martin, is in facilitating autonomy, mastery, and purpose for teachers; the teaching profession has been systematically deprofessionalized over the past several decades, and "reprofessionalization" is critical to the realization of the NGSS and the *Framework*.

INSTRUCTIONAL MATERIAL REVIEW PROCESS

> *How does the comprehensive instructional material review process support the continuum of instructional materials development, selection, adoption, and implementation? What are some examples of how those processes prioritize and support local needs for equity and social justice through adoption and implementation?*

Transitional Materials

New York state adopted its version of the standards in 2016, and New Visions for Public Schools was able to get funding to begin developing immediately usable transitional materials, said Kastel. One challenge, she said, was that state assessments hadn't changed, but teachers needed materials to get started with the transition. These first materials were intended to be three-dimensional, but not necessarily fully aligned to all the standards. She noted that they leveraged and built on models that teachers were already familiar with to mitigate the "re-novicing" effect of the NGSS. Professional learning and coaching were offered to support these transitional materials, Kastel said. As teachers began to develop expertise and comfort with the NGSS, the organization began developing fully aligned materials for the high school level.

New York is still in a transition zone, as state exams will not change until at least 2025. However, this time is critical for piloting, testing, and revising materials before everyone is held accountable to the new standards, she said. Both the transitional materials and the fully aligned materials are being supported simultaneously, to meet people where they are right now. Because implementation of new standards and materials does not work if teachers are doing it in isolation, the organization has been hosting ongoing leadership convenings to build support on all levels. To build capacity for wider-spread adoption of new materials, said Kastel, they are reaching past early adopters to build broader excitement and interest, and to help schools understand how the materials can support current state standards and exams.

Formal Review

In Oregon, said Rumage, the Department of Education conducts a formalized review of standards and instructional materials every seven years. These reviews are intended to ensure access to HQIM and reduce the time and financial burdens on districts. The Department works with an advisory panel to develop review criteria and a review process; the advisory panel is a mechanism for leveraging the expertise and professionalism of the state's educators. The review process is grounded in the Department's equity stance, as well as nationally developed science review criteria (e.g., EQuIP). Moving forward, said Rumage, there is an effort to focus on cultural relevance and cultural responsiveness of curricula and materials, so that "students are able to see themselves" in the work. It is critically important, she said, for students to see themselves in classroom materials, and also be able to peek into other worlds and see what it's like from someone else's perspective or lived experience.

Instructional Vision

Understanding the criteria for quality instructional materials, said Epler, begins with understanding the instructional vision for science education. It is critical, he said, that people at all layers in the system—from the superintendent to teachers—can understand and articulate the vision to make the best decisions. Martin added that teachers need the time and space not only to understand the vision but also to process, push back, debate, and dive into the issues around materials development and implementation. Any kind of implementation effort requires giving teachers the opportunity to have conversations, reflect, and plan collaboratively. In addition to these considerations, Bell said when decisions are being made about what materials to use or how to adapt them, it "matters who is at the table, who is in the room." Without a solid understanding of equity and the history of injustice, choices can "re-inscribe dominant views that have been in the field for far too long."

LASER Model

O'Donnell introduced workshop participants to the five pillars of the Smithsonian's Leadership and Assistance for Science Education Reform (LASER) model. The first pillar, she said, is identifying and building off of the local vision for instructional improvement. Second is selecting curricular or instructional materials that will support student learning experiences, and third is providing differentiated professional learning opportunities to educators. Fourth is providing leadership development opportunities and community engagement to build sustainable infrastructure. Finally, the fifth pillar is ensuring that assessments are aligned with the rest of the model. Currently, said O'Donnell, standards in every state "are local interpretations and derivatives" of the NGSS or another set of standards because "education is the responsibility of the state." However, there are a number of national review systems. Therefore, to achieve equity in education, there is a need for national review systems to be contextualized to ensure the best outcome for each individual student at the local level. There is a need to focus on designing materials that allow for local implementation and to build review systems that recognize the needs of the local context, she said. Furthermore, there is a need to build capacity within schools or districts to understand and contextualize national reviews. She noted that complex socioscientific issues, such as energy use or freshwater access, have to be locally adapted in order to be meaningful; facilitating local adaptation of science curriculum is "really more representative of how real science and real engineering work."

DISCUSSION

After the guided panel discussion, Shaw relayed questions from workshop participants to the panelists.

> *Where should the field go next, and where are the opportunities ahead?*

O'Donnell responded that prioritizing student experience is paramount. The implementation of the NGSS is "not easy," and instructional materials and built-in supports need to be designed as tools for implementing and localizing the NGSS in the classroom. While doing so, "we have to keep feasibility and usability in the back of our minds," she said, and need to balance the development of HQIM with the time it takes to actually implement them. The future of science education will be exploring complex, socioscientific issues on a local scale, using the community as a laboratory, while giving students the tools to act and use their education for the social good.

The NGSS gives us a platform to explore socioscientific issues such as the intersection of climate change with racial and class injustice, said Bell, but there is a need to go beyond the NGSS to consider the role of science and engineering in hyperlocal phenomena and community adaptation. This is a space where we need instructional materials that can build toward transformation. Kastel agreed with this need and said that there are discussions in New York of developing a justice-centered science course; the challenge, however, is funding these types of efforts.

For science to be prioritized, it is essential to improve communication with school administrators, said Martin. Although many great ideas have been discussed at this workshop, implementation of these ideas won't happen "unless we actually convince people that don't come to webinars like this that science education actually has value." Epler concurred that communication is critical and said that communication about science education and standards with parents, families, communities, and local board of education members needs improvement.

What is the role of professional development in the review of high-quality instructional materials?

A review of instructional materials "should be a form of professional learning," said Rumage. The process in itself is "an amazing way" of learning and understanding how instructional materials are structured and their purpose. Martin said that there is a tension between developing very comprehensive, lengthy materials, and meeting teachers where they are. There needs to be a focus on implementation, which requires "rolling up our sleeves" and helping teachers personalize material and collaborate with other educators to develop their capacity. O'Donnell added that thinking of teachers as learners during professional learning is crucial—even after 37 years in education, she said that she can learn so much by "going through it myself as a learner."

To what extent can national curriculum materials be effectively incorporated in preservice teacher preparation?

Teacher educators need to be part of these conversations, said Kastel. Some teacher educators, particularly adjunct faculty who teach early methods courses, are quite removed from the conversations of boots-on-the-ground educators. There are opportunities for cross-collaboration, she said; for example, the Master of Arts in Teaching program at the Museum of Natural History uses instructional materials that teachers may be able to use in the New York City school system. Unaligned preservice teacher education is a major challenge of coherent curriculum implementation, said Bell. Working in Washington state on a climate design collaborative, Bell has noticed that methods, opportunities, and formats are "wildly different across institutions," which can make it challenging to communicate and work together.

Epler said that there is a need for a mindset shift in teacher preparation around preservice teachers as developers of curriculum versus skillful users of HQIM. Preservice teachers are "not curriculum developers, nor should we expect them to be." Martin agreed and said that both preservice teachers and preservice teacher educators could benefit from opportunities to "adopt the student hat." Adopting the perspective of a student can allow educators to better understand how to accomplish the engagement with phenomena, desired outcomes, and performance expectations, he said.

8

Assessment as a "Caring Practice"—Systems of Assessment

The assessment journey for the NGSS, said Aneesha Badrinarayan (Learning Policy Institute), started at the very beginning; one of the immediate consequences of three-dimensional (3-D) standards is that they "pose a real disruption to the way that we have traditionally thought about assessment." However, assessment can serve as a guide for moving forward and thinking about meaningful teaching and learning, what information is useful to surface, and how to support teachers. "Assessment ultimately is about supporting student learning toward the goals that we have, and students have for themselves," she said.

Badrinarayan asked workshop participants to think about what they value most about the experiences that students have, the performance that they can produce as a result of their educational experiences, and what role assessment plays in meeting this vision. When people are asked these questions, she said, they tend to focus on students seeing themselves and their identities as essential components of the scientific endeavor, on students building confidence and growing, and on students becoming critical thinkers who can navigate complex novel situations. What people generally don't focus on, said Badrinarayan, is content memorization or knowing rote steps for a procedure without understanding the context or how to apply their knowledge. A major part of the assessment journey for the NGSS has been reconsidering how we match up what we want to cultivate and support in students with what our assessments are monitoring.

Since 2014, when the Board on Testing and Assessment (BOTA) and Board on Science Education (BOSE) released the report on *Developing Assessments for the Next Generation Science Standards*, there has been "a real journey" of figuring out what assessment should look like and identifying the kinds of tools and resources that teachers and students need in the classroom. As time has gone on, criteria have been released to help us think about what high-quality assessments look like, she said, and there has been an evolution toward looking at assessment through an equity lens. Most recently, there has been a call to action to elevate science assessments in local and federal accountability processes, as well as to start to think about the use of assessment for students and teachers in the classroom. This represents a shift away from thinking about assessment as large-scale tests and toward assessment as a "wraparound support for all the teaching and learning goals that we have for students." Resources have been developed, such as learning communities, implementation and design tools, and models to learn from. This work has led to some common "non-negotiable" features of 3-D science assessment, said Badrinarayan, to include the following: focused on figuring out phenomena and problems, requiring sensemaking with ideas and practices, and equitable and fair to students.

Through all this work, "we know a lot more about what we want assessments to look like and do," she said. This panel will continue this work by considering the successes we have had in implementing the vision, what tools have been useful, and what opportunities there are to keep progressing. Badrinarayan cautioned that the discussion would not focus on which assessment is the "best one" but would instead look broadly at where we are and how to move forward. Like in the other sessions, Badrinarayan asked the following five panelists a series of questions.

- Daniel Alcazar-Roman, The Lawrence Hall of Science at the University of California, Berkeley
- Alec Barron, San Diego Science Project
- Tamara "TJ" Heck, Michigan Department of Education
- Angela Landrum, Colorado Department of Education
- Jim Pellegrino, University of Illinois at Chicago

VISION FOR ASSESSMENT

What does it look like for students to demonstrate learning and performance as laid out by the Framework and the NGSS?

One of the challenges of developing assessments that are aligned to the NGSS, said Pellegrino, is that a lot of priority is given to classroom assessment. That is, teachers need tasks to give students to monitor their progress toward meeting performance expectations. Pellegrino shared a video of three seventh-grade girls engaged in solving an assessment task that was developed by the Next Generation Science Assessment group, a collaborative that has been working to develop tasks for the classroom. This task was designed to get the students to construct a scientific explanation using evidence that describes the patterns of organisms interacting in different ways, he explained. The students have previously had instruction related to this performance expectation in class and received a prompt to help them solve the task collaboratively. These types of tasks are freely available to educators in an online portal;[1] he noted that there have been more than 1 million page views, nearly 10,000 teachers have registered on the site, and the site has been accessed by users from 153 different countries.

"I am one of those users," said Barron, saying that the San Diego Science Project has been supporting collaborative inquiry and sensemaking through tasks such as the one that Pellegrino shared. The key, he said, is making these performances visible not just to the teachers but also to the students so that they can monitor their progress with learning. Although there has already been quite a bit of work on long cycle assessments and end-of-learning tests, the next frontier of work is to focus on short cycle assessment processes that help support students with moving toward goals. In Barron's former role as a content specialist, he used three core questions to guide student assessment: Where am I with my learning, where am I headed, and how am I going to get there?

Badrinarayan asked the panelists to elaborate on how teachers would use tasks such as the one Pellegrino shared. Pellegrino said that these tasks were deliberately designed to be used by teachers embedded in the context of their ongoing instructional plan. They are not stand-alone projects but instead are used purposefully to get evidence about how the students are doing. A teacher can also build off these tasks to stimulate conversation about the thinking process and the context of how the task fits into the larger curriculum. Pellegrino said that it is really important to understand that assessment is intended to be linked to ongoing curriculum and instruction, "not apart from it."

CLASSROOM-LEVEL ASSESSMENT

What are some best practices for classroom assessment, and what are some challenges that are emerging as we consider how to support students and teachers?

[1] http://nextgenscienceassessment.org/task-portal/.

In Barron's work in Escondido, California, the teachers asked a novel question: "If the NGSS is framing for us a new vision for student learning, then shouldn't that mean we have a new vision for assessment to support these learning experiences?" One of the great areas of progress that the field has made in this area, he said, is in creating tools like the Achieve Science Task Screener and protocols from the Center for Collaborative Education. These developments have supported the work of re-professionalizing educators to engage in classroom assessment of students. For example, said Barron, one powerful tool that came out of the work of professional learning communities was tuning protocols with rubrics to support students with more specific and actionable feedback. In terms of challenges, Barron said there is sometimes too much focus on longer cycle assessments rather than shorter cycle assessments. There is a need to develop tools and resources to support short-cycle formative processes in actual learning contexts, he said. Barron shared that he and his partners have been working to develop an NGSS assessment toolkit to bring greater coherence among curriculum, instruction, and assessment at the classroom level.

In Colorado, said Landrum, graduating students are required to pass one or more assessments from a menu of options; the menu includes traditional assessments such as the ACT and SAT but also innovative student-centered options such as capstones and performance assessments. The vision for the performance assessment component, she said, is to create a pathway for all students to connect what they learned in the classroom to their experiences as individuals in a way that leads to a more authentic and sophisticated application of knowledge and skill. Assessment is an essential component of effective implementation of the NGSS, and Landrum and her colleagues have been building resources and guidance for high-quality performance assessment. One of the first resources that they developed was a set of design elements to serve as criteria for what is considered high-quality performance assessment. The design elements include features common to NGSS implementation, such as alignment of content, skills, cognitive complexity, accessibility for all learners, authenticity, relevancy, and transferability. One unique feature, said Landrum, is that performance assessment be iterative, to connect it closely to the classroom. The collaborative protocols for this work are critical and serve to elevate the quality of the assessment by establishing "what it looks like when students are successful."

Landrum listed several challenges that have been identified through this work. High school is "notorious" for being siloed, she said, so establishing coherence both vertically and horizontally can be difficult. District and school leaders sometimes express support for this work, but they don't help remove the barriers for teachers or are unable to articulate how the work aligns and supports school and district goals. This lack of support from leaders can leave teachers feeling isolated and undervalued; consequently, the professional learning efforts that teachers are involved in may not have the desired impact on educator practice and student outcomes. Landrum said that recent research has surfaced the need for systematic approaches to professional learning for teachers. In the absence of high-quality examples, "many educators really believe that the work that they're doing is meeting expectations when in fact it is not." These challenges are being addressed through work with the State Performance Assessment Learning Community, which provides educators with curriculum-embedded or curriculum-anchored assessment supports, and helps teachers design and use assessment with support, coaching, and connection with educators across the country. This is particularly helpful, she said, for educators in rural areas; feeling a sense of coherence and camaraderie with teachers in other areas is "really valuable."

Alcazar-Roman gave his perspective on where progress is being made in this area. Educators are now collaborating to design assessments rather than working in isolation, and more principled approaches, such as evidence-centered design, are being used to guide assessment and development at the classroom and local level. For example, he said, in Washington, DC, modules from the Access Project were used to help teachers understand the NGSS and assessment; at the same time, teachers were engaged in the process of developing learning performances for every performance expectation that is included in state-level science assessments. Teachers spent many months deeply engaging in understanding the standards, unpacking the dimensions, and building maps to guide the development of assessments. As a result, groups of teachers in DC are getting together to use the same evidence-centered design to build their own assessments. In this process, said Alcazar-Roman, it was critical to go beyond teachers and involve the local education community. For example, the Smithsonian Science Education Center helped with engaging teachers in looking at claims for assessment, reporting, and figuring out local phenomena to include. There is great value in teachers, practitioners, and researchers collaborating to develop tools to work toward better assessments, said Alcazar-Roman.

ROLE OF THE STATE

What role are states playing to impact practice at the local level in positive ways?

One of the biggest projects undertaken in Michigan, said Heck, is an effort to develop a new state science assessment with a variety of partners.

Michigan has always involved local educators in the writing and reviewing of assessment tasks, but with the NGSS, there was a need to bring on and partner with people who had different kinds of knowledge, including classroom teachers and science education researchers. This collaboration brought together multiple perspectives of practice and research in the design space for large-scale assessment, she said. In addition, the collaboration offered opportunities for networking, professional learning, and building relationships between researchers and practitioners. Another state-led effort, said Heck, has been facilitating a shift away from rote knowledge practices toward phenomenon-focused assessment structures; this allows students to use their sensemaking skills and bring together their knowledge of various dimensions of knowledge on the assessment. Heck joked, "If you can Google it, it doesn't belong on my test." The vision is to move the large-scale assessment toward what we want to see happening in the classroom, she said. Although people "cringe" at the idea of teaching to the test, Heck said that her goal has been to create a test that is worth teaching to.

Colorado only recently adopted NGSS-aligned standards, and implementation began in the 2021 school year, said Landrum. Most of the educators in the state are still figuring out what it looks like to teach and assess in ways that are aligned with and appropriate for the NGSS, and educators are working to build consensus on what will be expected of students. Although the implementation of the NGSS is still very much in progress, Colorado is working to enable meaningful systems of assessment conversation. Landrum said that the state is providing guidance, examples, and guardrails for how classrooms and districts can generate evidence to move student learning forward. The state assessment is considered only one small piece of the comprehensive assessment system, she said, and it is not expected to capture all learning in science. Landrum and her colleagues at the state level are working tirelessly to bring teachers and leaders into the conversation about appropriate and intentional use of assessment across the system.

PROGRESS ON ASSESSMENT SYSTEMS

What kind of progress is being made on assessment systems for the NGSS, and how does implementation compare to the theory that guided the development of the NGSS?

We always knew it was going to be a challenge to develop assessments for the NGSS, said Pellegrino, due to the nature of the standards, as well as the state of assessment design. Other speakers, he said, have noted the need for a system of assessments that are coherent with each other, aligned to the same vision and goals, and designed for particular purposes. The BOTA/BOSE report on NGSS assessments discusses the need for both formative and summative classroom assessments, and the fact that state monitoring assessments cannot be "drop-in from the sky" large-scale assessments. Landrum and Heck both illustrated the need for assessments that are tuned to the particular context and purpose, he said. Even at the state level, it is important to not rely entirely on year-end large-scale assessments but to instead use smaller-scale classroom assessments that involve performance tasks. One of the biggest challenges, said Pellegrino, is supporting teachers in understanding exactly what these kinds of assessments look like in practice and how to support students in reaching the goals that are set. The large-scale state test is oftentimes the "boogieman" in the process, he said, but it can lead to positive change by signifying the kinds of things that we want students to be able to do.

EQUITY AND ASSESSMENTS

What progress has been made on embedding equity into assessments? What challenges remain?

"When I first came into this position," said Heck, "I started digging around" and asking colleagues what was happening regarding equity and large-scale assessment. The response, she said, was "crickets in the room." We have come a long way in the past several years in considering equity and assessment by prioritizing assessments where students need to use sensemaking rather than rote memorization or high-level language skills. These are the kinds of deterrents, she said, that can prevent students from having the opportunity to show us what they know and can do in science. Another important step being taken is ensuring that phenomena that are presented on large-scale assessments are relevant and palatable to students.

At the state level in Michigan, a bias and sensitivity review committee examines each assessment item, and stakeholders with specific lenses (e.g., special education, English language learner) look for potential issues. Although this process is important, said Heck, it is not enough. It is critical to get people on these committees who are representative of our students. For example, in Michigan, meetings tend to be held on the lower peninsula, which results in a lack of representation from the rural upper peninsula. In addition, said Heck, there is a need to find a way to involve students in the assessment development and design process to get the perspective of the people for whom the assessment is designed. Finally, Heck said that as we bring more diverse groups of people into the space of assessment development, we need to offer professional learning opportunities around issues like microaggressions, anti-racist training, and cultural diversity education.

Alcazar-Roman agreed that there is a need for more action on equity at the state level; in particular, he noted that bias and sensitivity reviews are the last step in the process rather than embedding equity along the entire path of assessment development. Pellegrino agreed with this point and said that we need to "think about equity from the very outset of design." He added that equity be considered when identifying performance expectations, relevant phenomena, and potential linguistic challenges; waiting until the assessment has been developed is too "late in the game." Although improvements are being made in this area, large-scale assessments are by their nature going to have a degree of decontextualization because of the need to homogenize assessments for a large group of students, Pellegrino said. Despite this challenge, he said "we still have to strive to make it as fair and equitable as possible."

On the bright side, Alcazar-Roman said, there is a lot of investment in the world of large-scale assessment, which means the opportunity to leverage funds to meet the vision of equity. In DC, they have undertaken several efforts in this area, including identifying more local phenomena, reconsidering how to design problems, and building models of universal design. There is further work to do, said Alcazar-Roman, such as looking at social and environmental justice issues in the assessments. State- and federal-level assessments tend to have a number of restrictions, but at the classroom and district levels, there is more flexibility for adapting assessments to the context of the learner. We need tools to help educator networks contextualize phenomenon and problems and develop tasks that address local issues so that assessments can be more culturally relevant and equitable, Alcazar-Roman said. Doing so will enable students not only to demonstrate their science knowledge but also to see how they can make a difference and solve problems in the community. Furthermore, said Alcazar-Roman, there is a need to diversify the people involved in education and assessment—we need the people making decisions and development assessments for millions of students to match the diversity of those students.

DISCUSSION

Participant question: How does assessment relate to the practice of grading?

When using assessment in a formative way, said Pellegrino, scores and grading should not be part of the process. Instead, he added, the feedback should be aligned with the kinds of thinking that we want students to be able to do. However, part of the challenge is that grading is embedded in teachers' assessment, literacy, and ongoing practices, he said. Heck added that we need to consider "who is grading serving" and how we can create a system that will actually be of value to the parents and students in providing feedback. One approach, she said, is to create a student learning story—how are the students learning and growing, and what can they do now that they couldn't before?

9

Tools and Resources to Build Capacity and Drive Coherence

In this session, workshop participants divided into four breakout groups to discuss tools and resources geared toward building capacity and driving coherence for standards implementation. In these sessions, participants were asked to discuss the strengths, weaknesses, and opportunities in these areas. After the breakout groups concluded, workshop participants reconvened and provided brief synopses of their conversations, which were followed by a question-and-answer session. The four breakout groups were as follows:

1. Preschool to Elementary Transition
2. Curriculum and Instructional Materials
3. Formative Assessment
4. Instructional Practice

PRESCHOOL TO ELEMENTARY TRANSITION

One of the top strengths of the early childhood education (ECE) space is that it is more unconstrained than the K–12 setting, said Andres Bustamante (University of California, Irvine) (see Figure 9-1). Many K–12 educators report feeling beholden to a certain curriculum and worrying about high-stakes testing, whereas in the ECE space there is more opportunity to create exploration and hands-on playful learning. Many ECE teachers are already engaged in high-quality practices, such as open-ended questions and inquiry cycles, that are ideal for three-dimensional (3-D) science learning, he said. ECE providers also tend to use observational assessments to

Strengths

What resources do we have?

- Pre-K is more unconstrained than K-12
- High quality ECE practice is what we strive for in K-12 settings
- ECE has deep connections to community (faith based organizations, home-based care) and diverse ecosystems to support early development

What is working well?

- Early spaces do a good job using observational assessment (K-12 can learn from this)
- Families are a main driver of early science
- Family participation is common and a central focus

Weaknesses

What resources/tools are we lacking?

- Because there is so much variability in ECE providers it's difficult to provide comprehensive PD for all of the audiences
- Pushing down K-12 practices to ECE instead of the opposite
- Lack of science in ECE (teachers sometimes opt into ECE to avoid science)

What improvements could be made?

- Messaging to ECE educators and parents that they have expertise in early science (question asking, inquiry, language modeling) and it only takes minor tweaks to create 3D science learning
- Need for policy coherence in the connection between pre-K and K-12 worlds

Opportunities

What are best possible next steps?

- Practices and crosscutting concepts lend themselves particularly well to high-quality ECE instructional practices
- Lots of opportunity to support students' identity and build from their cultural funds of knowledge because of the deep connections with families and community organizations
- Parent and family engagement are highly encouraged and there is a lot of thought behind highlighting that science is everywhere and that many of families' existing practices are scientific

FIGURE 9-1 Summary of Preschool to Elementary Transition Breakout Group Discussion reported by Andres Bustamante.
NOTE: PD = professional development.

examine the quality of their practices, organization, and environment. K–12 could benefit from incorporating similar holistic assessment approaches that use some of these observational protocols, said Bustamante.

Another strength of ECE is its deep connections to community, such as faith-based organizations and home-based care. Even in publicly funded ECE, there is a focus on family engagement and building connections between home and school. Furthermore, said Bustamante, there is a diverse ecosystem of ECE providers, which allows children to see themselves and their culture in learning environments. This is something that "we really strive for" in K–12, he said.

One challenge in the ECE space, however, is the huge amount of variability in ECE providers, including state-funded pre–Ks, Head Start, faith-based groups, private businesses, and families. The education and training of individual providers varies widely, and there are a wide variety of settings and environments. Bustamante said that this makes it difficult to provide high-level supports or professional development opportunities for ECE providers. Another challenge, he said, is the unfortunate trend of K–12 practices being pushed down to ECE rather than the other way around. He explained that some ECE spaces, particularly those that serve children in underresourced neighborhoods and/or Black and Brown children, can get "caught up in some of the same pitfalls" of focusing on rote learning and memorization. Bustamante emphasized the need for building on the strengths of what ECE does well rather than pushing it to look more like K–12 education.

To capitalize on the strengths and opportunities within ECE, Bustamante said there is a need to convey to parents and teachers that many of them are already "doing science"; some minor tweaks and support could help ECE educators make explicit connections between their existing practices and 3-D science education. There are many opportunities to build upon students' cultural funds of knowledge due to the deep connections between ECE and families and communities, and the unconstrained nature of the ECE space means that providers can use a "science is everywhere" approach.

CURRICULUM AND INSTRUCTIONAL MATERIALS

As discussed earlier in the workshop, said Christine Cunningham (Pennsylvania State University), there are several high-quality instructional materials that exist, and the number is growing (see Figure 9-2). There are rubrics and review processes and tools available, districts are acting as resources for one another, and materials have been developed that are relevant to local communities and cultures. Some materials are free and open access, and there are efforts to connect resources and professional learning opportunities across communities.

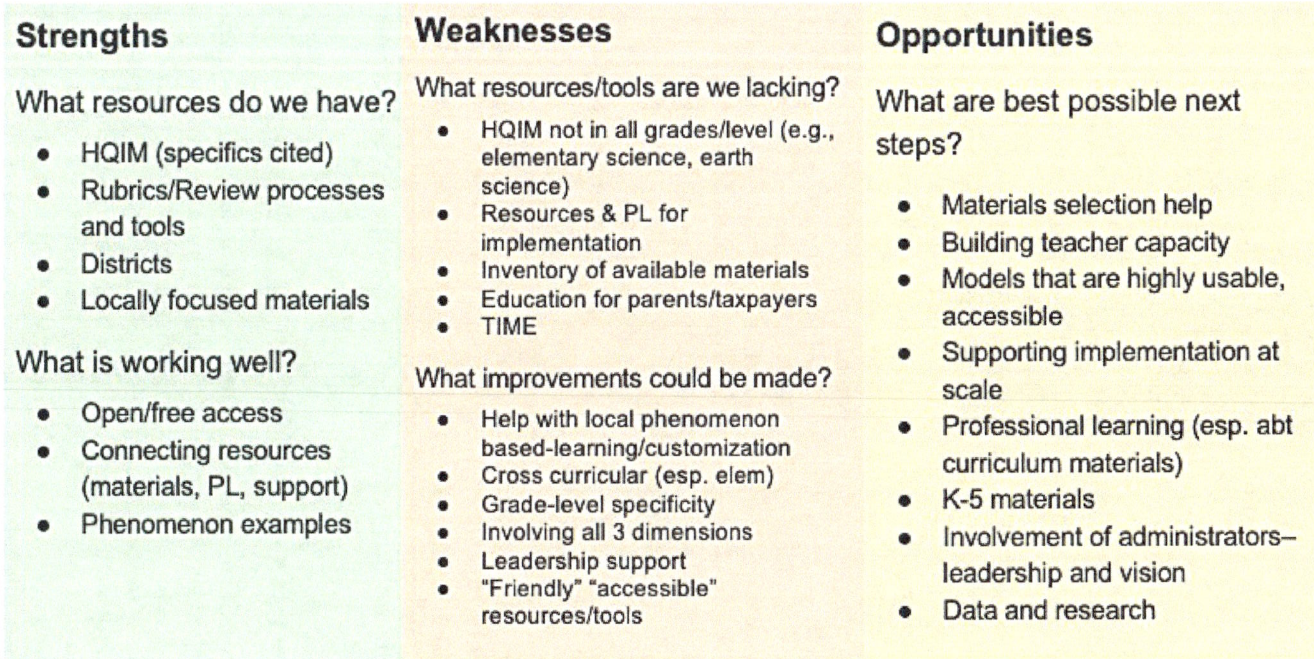

FIGURE 9-2 Summary of Curriculum and Instructional Materials Breakout Group Discussion reported by Christine Cunningham.
NOTE: HQIM = High-quality instructional materials; PL = professional learning.

The weaknesses in this area, said Cunningham, include a lack of tools and resources in certain areas. For example, elementary schools are sorely in need of additional resources, and there is a lack of materials for topics such as earth science. To fully implement the vision of the *Framework* and the NGSS, she said, there is a need for additional resources and professional learning opportunities; furthermore, teachers need dedicated time for learning, teaching, and planning. The breakout group had two innovative ideas to address weaknesses in this area. The first was to develop an inventory of what materials and resources are already developed to reduce duplicative efforts and increase collaboration and sharing. The second idea, said Cunningham, was to educate parents, taxpayers, and policy makers around the importance of the NGSS and the need for funds and time to implement the vision. Other needs that were identified by the breakout group included support for developing local phenomenon-based learning, cross-curricular materials, grade-level specific materials, and materials that are "friendly and accessible" to both educators and students. A workshop participant added that while the development of specific types of material is essential, it is critical to remember that material is part of a larger system that is coherent and aligned.

The group identified several immediate needs in the area of instructional materials including the following:

- Help with selecting materials
- Efforts to build teacher capacity
- Models that are highly usable and accessible
- Support for implementation at scale
- Professional learning about curriculum materials
- Materials for K–5 classrooms
- Involvement and buy-in from leadership and administrators
- Further data and research to help guide decision making

FORMATIVE ASSESSMENT

In the area of formative assessment, there are a number of examples to look at and information to learn from, said Sara Cooper (Independent Consultant) (see Figure 9-3). There are specific tools that teachers can implement in classrooms, such as routines that make space to reveal student sensemaking. Professional learning communities have been formed to allow teachers to collaborate and learn together, while research-practice partnerships are moving science forward in classrooms. Strategies that are used in classroom instruction are also being applied to professional learning opportunities for educators, administrators, and leaders.

However, despite this progress, said Cooper, there are notable weak-

Strengths

What resources do we have?

- **Examples** to look at and learn from (e.g., OER resources)
- **Information** to learn from and apply generally in local contexts (e.g., STEM Teaching Tools)
- Specific **routines** that create space to reveal student sense-making

What is working well?

- **Professional Learning Communities** that allow teachers to collaborate and learn together
- **Research Practice Partnerships**
- Using tools and resources across a variety of contexts (e.g., routines, use of phenomena)

Weaknesses

What resources/tools are we lacking?

- Resources that support **localization** in ways that are usable (e.g., guidance and support for quality feedback, communication tools for all system shareholders)
- Deep understanding of **assessment literacy** and the role of and importance of formative assessment
- Robust examples/resources that demonstrate appropriate interpretation, use, adaptation based on evidence, and articulated instructional next steps

What improvements could be made?

- **Coherence** across PK-16 systems
- Attention to **student-centered** assessment systems that attend to equity
- **Usability** of and accessibility to formative assessment resources

Opportunities

What are best possible next steps?

- Working directly with instructional materials developers
  - This can be an avenue to adaptation processes
- Usability of formative assessment materials (e.g., one-pagers)
- Rethinking the role of formative assessment in the criteria for high-quality instructional materials (built-in guidance for meaningful use of formative assessment)

FIGURE 9-3 Summary of Formative Assessment Breakout Group Discussion reported on by Sara Cooper.
NOTE: OER = open educational resources.

nesses. There is a lack of resources that support adaptation and localization of existing tools and resources; for example, there is a need for guidance and support for quality feedback, and communication tools for all system shareholders. There are areas of improvement around assessment literacy, particularly the role and importance of formative assessment in classrooms and the system as a whole. In addition, there is a need for more robust examples to demonstrate the appropriate use of formative assessment, how assessments can be adapted for local context, and articulated instructional next steps. Cooper said that improvements are needed in three specific areas: coherence across pre-K–16 systems, attention to student-centered assessment systems that attend to equity, and usability of and accessibility to formative assessment resources. Cooper noted that "boots-on-the-ground" teachers may not have access to materials or may not understand how best to use them; this may be particularly true for teachers who are isolated. One pressing need is to develop usable formative assessment materials such as one-pagers, to get these resources in the hands of educators. Other immediate needs include considering how to closely connect curriculum, instruction, and assessment, and working directly with instructional materials developers to build coherence across the system.

INSTRUCTIONAL PRACTICE

There are a great number of resources available for instructional practice, said Kate McNeill (Boston College), as well as professional organizations that are facilitating collaboration and sharing (see Figure 9-4). Teachers are becoming more aware of the need to use locally relevant phenomena in instruction, and when teachers are provided with the necessary time and opportunities for professional learning, "amazing work" is being done in classrooms. Time, however, remains a challenge, said McNeill. There is a lack of time dedicated to science instruction and planning in the K–12 setting; "if we want teachers to be doing this instructional shift, we need to give them time to engage in it." In addition to time, a lack of funding is another challenge that constrains implementation of the NGSS.

The group identified several areas for improvement. There is a need to get all educators on the same page, with a common vision, and to build support from administrators and key stakeholders at all levels. There is a need to continue conversations with multiple voices and multiple perspectives to learn from one another, share resources, and learn how to adapt and adopt models and materials. Much work has been done since the publication of the *Framework* and the NGSS, said McNeill, and there are opportunities to continue to build on this success, particularly around equity. Importantly, we need to care and support teachers in their work. "Teaching has always

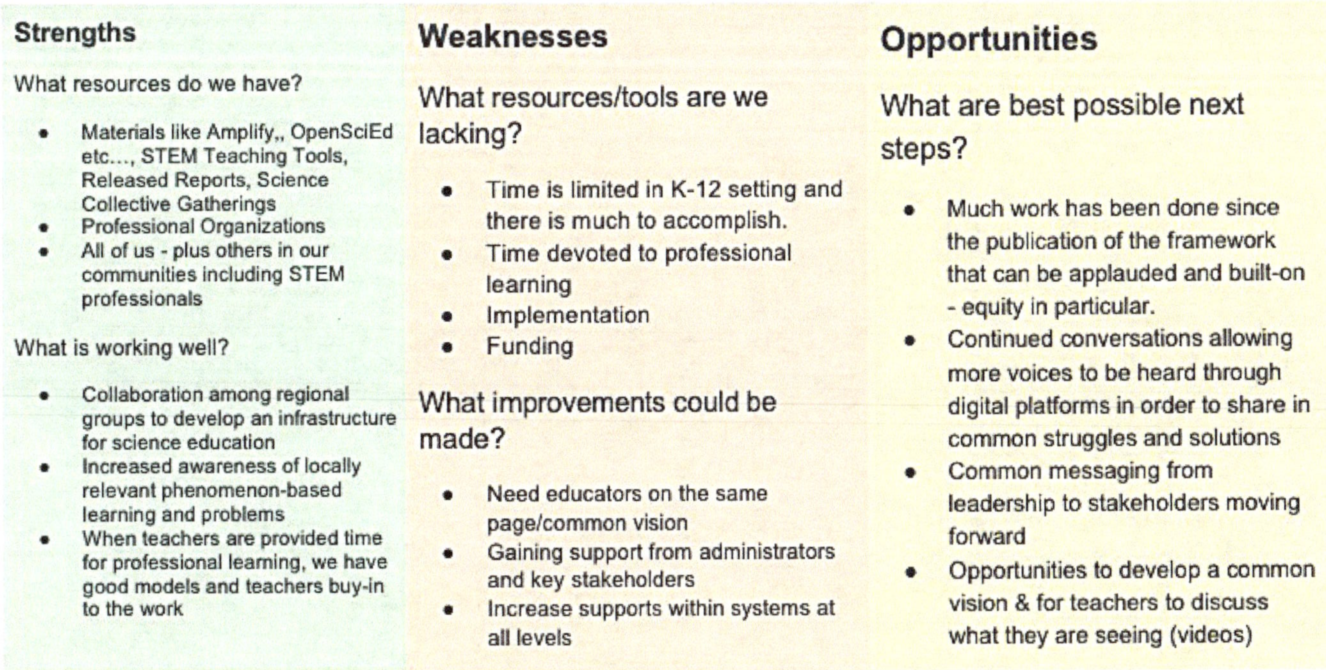

FIGURE 9-4 Summary of Instructional Practice Breakout Group Discussion reported by Kate McNeill.

been hard, and it is particularly hard right now," said McNeill, and teachers need time, support, and resources to do their important work.

There were three categories of needs that the group identified as urgent and important, said McNeill. First was systems and infrastructure: there is a need to elevate science to the forefront and develop a shared vision across schools, districts, states, and other stakeholders. Second was time: time provided for teachers and other stakeholders to engage in professional learning as a community to support these shifts. The third category was equity: equity needs to be at the center with a focus on what equitable science instruction looks like; for example, rather than focusing on scientific language, hearing and supporting the "brilliance that youth bring to the classroom." As an example, McNeill shared a quote from a middle school science student who felt like part of the scientific endeavor and focused on the collaborative nature of inquiry: "We were the ones who came up with it, so we were able to understand. We had similar ideas or different ideas. So, we were able to come up with this one model that we could ALL understand because WE came up with it."

10

Reflections and Possible Next Steps

Each workshop day ended with a final session in which planning committee members offered their reflections, discussed main takeaways, and identified themes that cropped up repeatedly during the day. Below is a synopsis of these sessions. On the final day, Garcia discussed the next steps for both the field generally, as well as the workshop series specifically.

REFLECTIONS

One common theme throughout the Summit, said Duncan, was that there is a lack of time for teachers to engage in this work. Professional development, learning, and planning are things that often have to be done "on the side." It is critical, she said, that we center these needs of teachers, and that professional development is driven by the needs and the assets of students and communities. Shaw added that time is limited, yet professional learning in a variety of topics and skills is essential. He suggested that there be efforts to integrate professional learning across disciplines and areas to maximize the time that is available. Badrinarayan echoed this, noting that there is a tendency for experts to "burrow" into their field rather than look for opportunities to collaborate and share. She observed that discussions that were focused on one implementation lever (e.g., assessment) often diverged into discussions of other implementation levers because of the interconnected nature. Badrinarayan wondered aloud how the field could leverage common resources and approaches to advance practice across sectors rather than focusing on any one area. Olivares summed up the need for collaboration and integration by saying, "If this is worth doing, then we should do it together."

Committee members also noted the importance of keeping diversity and equity at the forefront of the work. Shelton emphasized the need to include more diverse voices, including student voices, when working to implement the vision, and Duncan added that curriculum and assessment be centered on students and their local contexts, without "closing doors to other contexts and situations" that may be interesting to them. Furthermore, said Duncan, although there are many available examples for curriculum and assessment, there are fewer examples of teaching with a focus on pushing the envelope on equity and justice. There is a need, she said, to give practitioners, administrators, and other stakeholders concrete examples of what equitable science education looks like. Suárez called for intentional diversification of the teacher workforce and said that if classrooms continue to lack diverse perspectives and voices, the implementation of equitable science education will be a challenge.

Several committee members noted that there are gaps in communication that are preventing existing resources and tools from reaching their intended audience. For example, said Duncan, there are great examples of curriculum materials and professional development that are available, but we have not done "a very good job marketing" because many people don't know about them. Sampson agreed, saying that even as somebody who is well-versed in the field, it is challenging to disseminate ideas and resources. Research papers are generally published a year or two after the work has been done, he said, so how do we "learn from each other in ways that are more timely?" In particular, how can ideas and resources be shared with people who are working in schools or systems that serve different communities? Shelton added that the intersection among policy, research, and practice can be "beautiful" and "powerful" in advancing change, but that it is critical to ensure that diverse voices are captured in this work.

POSSIBLE NEXT STEPS

Garcia thanked all the panelists, moderators, planning committee members, and workshop participants for a robust and fascinating conversation over the three days. One thing that particularly stood out, said Garcia, is the value of working in community and across sectors. Part of working in community, she said, is ensuring that the voices around the table are diverse and reflective of the community; this means including voices such as those from research, practice, parents, family members, students, community members, and state leaders. Garcia observed that there were many voices present at this workshop, but that there was likely a deficit of people such as administrators and school board members. She asked, "How do we invite folks who typically do not see this as their space into our space and into community with us?"

Garcia urged workshop participants to continue the conversations from the workshop and to advocate for science education not only in the systems in which they work but also in the policy sphere and their local communities. Garcia described the future activities of the Taking Stock of Science Standards Implementation Summit. A series of coffee talks will be held in the spring of 2022; each talk will cover a specific topic such as rural implementation or teacher preparation pathways. A final workshop will be held in April 2022 to reflect on the previous discussions and consider next steps, she said. Garcia thanked everyone for participating in the Summit and adjourned the meeting.

References

Banilower, E.R., Smith, P.S., Malzahn, K.A., Plumley, C.L., Gordon, E.M., and Hayes, M.L. (2018). *Report of the 2018 NSSME+*. Chapel Hill, NC: Horizon Research, Inc.

Bell, P., Campanella, M., and Rhinehart, A. (2022). Landscape survey analysis of equity-focused science education across PK–12 [conference presentation]. *National Association for Research in Science Teaching (NARST) 95th Annual International Conference*, Vancouver.

Calabrese Barton, A., and Tan, E. (2020). Beyond equity as inclusion: A framework for "rightful presence" for guiding justice-oriented studies in teaching and learning. *Educational Researcher, 49*(6), 433–440. https://doi.org/10.3102/0013189X20927363.

Calabrese Barton, A., and Tan, E. (2021). Designing for social justice in science teaching and learning: Working toward rightful presence. *NSTA Blog*. https://www.nsta.org/blog/designing-social-justice-science-teaching-and-learning-working-toward-rightful-presence.

Calabrese Barton, A., Tan, E., and Birmingham, D.J. (2020). Rethinking high-leverage practices in justice-oriented ways. *Journal of Teacher Education, 71*(4), 477–494. https://doi.org/10.1177/0022487119900209.

Campbell, T., and Lee, O. (2021). Instructional materials designed for *A Framework for K–12 Science Education* and the Next Generation Science Standards: An introduction to the special issue. *Journal of Science Teacher Education, 32*(7), 727–734. https://doi.org/10.1080/1046560X.2021.1975359.

EdReports. (2021). *K–12 Science Materials*. https://storage.googleapis.com/edreports-dev.appspot.com/media/2021/11/science-data-notes_FINAL_Nov2021.pdf.

National Academies of Sciences, Engineering, and Medicine (NASEM). (2018). *Design, Selection, and Implementation of Instructional Materials for the Next Generation Science Standards: Proceedings of a Workshop*. Washington, DC: The National Academies Press. https://doi.org/10.17226/25001.

NASEM. (2019). *Science and Engineering for Grades 6–12: Investigation and Design at the Center*. Washington, DC: The National Academies Press. https://doi.org/10.17226/25216.

NASEM. (2021). *Call to Action for Science Education: Building Opportunity for the Future*. Washington, DC: The National Academies Press. https://doi.org/10.17226/26152.

NASEM. (2022). *Science and Engineering in Preschool Through Elementary Grades: The Brilliance of Children and the Strengths of Educators.* Washington, DC: The National Academies Press. https://doi.org/10.17226/26215.

National Research Council (NRC). (2006). *America's Lab Report: Investigations in High School Science.* Washington, DC: The National Academies Press. https://doi.org/10.17226/11311.

NRC. (2012). *A Framework for K–12 Science Education: Practices, Crosscutting Concepts, and Core Ideas.* Washington, DC: The National Academies Press. https://doi.org/10.17226/13165.

NRC. (2014). *Developing Assessments for the Next Generation Science Standards.* Washington, DC: The National Academies Press. https://doi.org/10.17226/18409.

NRC. (2015). *Guide to Implementing the Next Generation Science Standards.* Washington, DC: The National Academies Press. https://doi.org/10.17226/18802.

NGSS Lead States. (2013). *Next Generation Science Standards: For States, By States.* Washington, DC: The National Academies Press. https://doi.org/10.17226/18290.

Rodriguez, A.J. (2015). What about a dimension of engagement, equity, and diversity practices? A critique of the Next Generation Science Standards. *Journal of Research in Science Teaching, 52,* 1031–1051. https://doi.org/10.1002/tea.21232.

Appendix A

Workshop Agenda

Taking Stock of Science Standards Implementation: A Summit

All Times are ET

Goals

The Board on Science Education (BOSE) of the National Academies of Sciences, Engineering, and Medicine (the National Academies) will host a public summit to take stock of the implementation of state science standards and determine the next steps for continuing or reinvigorating implementation efforts. The summit will serve as a setting to consider implementation across all states and territories, identify successes and challenges, and identify areas where additional resources or work is needed.

At the end of the summit, attendees will....

1. Understand the current state of science standards implementation.
2. Identify what needs to happen in the next phase of implementation.
3. Identify the tools, resources, and capital needed to advance a more just, equitable, and inclusive learning experience for our youth, teachers, and communities.

DAY 1: THURSDAY, OCTOBER 14TH

11:00 am	**Welcome and Summit Overview** Heidi Schweingruber, *Director, Board on Science Education, National Academies of Sciences, Engineering, and Medicine* Taunya Nesin, *Bill & Melinda Gates Foundation* Maya Garcia (*Chair*), *Colorado Department of Education*
11:30 am	**Plenary Session: *From Vision to Reality*** **Moderator:** Heidi Schweingruber, *BOSE, National Academies* **Virtual Moderator:** Sam Shaw, *EdReports.org* **Panelists:** • Philip Bell, *University of Washington* • Elizabeth A. (Betsy) Davis, *University of Michigan* • Michael Lach, *Assistant Superintendent of Curriculum, Instruction, and Assessment at Township High School District 113* • Tiffany Neill, *Oklahoma State Department of Education*
12:10 pm	**Discussion/Q&A with panelists**
12:40 pm	**Break**
1:15 pm	**Panel: *The Landscape of Implementation*** **Moderator:** Maya Garcia, *Colorado Department of Education* **Virtual Moderator:** Jessica Henderson-Rockette, *Instruction Partners* **Panelists:** • Stefanie Marshall, *University of Minnesota* • Bill Penuel, *University of Colorado Boulder* • Jenny Sarna, *NextGenScience WestEd* • Jim Spillane, *Northwestern University*
1:55 pm	**Discussion/Q&A with panelists**
2:15 pm	**Break**

3:00 pm **Panel:** ***The Role(s) of Leadership***
Moderators: James Blake, *Lincoln Public Schools*
Virtual Moderator: Aneesha Badrinarayan, *Learning Policy Institute*

Panelists:
- Gudiel Crosthwaite, *Superintendent, Lynwood Unified School District*
- Zoe Evans, *Principal, Bowdon High School*
- Mike Heinz, *Science Coordinator, New Jersey Department of Education, President of Council of State Science Supervisors*
- Elizabeth Mulkerrin, *Omaha Zoo and Aquarium, NSTA President Elect*
- Takako Olson, *Director of Curriculum, Lincoln Public Schools*

3:40 pm **Discussion/Q&A with panelists**

4:00 pm **Open Discussion:** *Reflections on the day*
Facilitator: Maya Garcia, *Colorado Department of Education*

4:30 pm **Wrap up and Adjourn**
Maya Garcia (*Chair*), *Colorado Department of Education*

DAY 2: FRIDAY, OCTOBER 15TH

11:00 am **Welcome, Day 1 Overview, and Preview of Day 2**
Heidi Schweingruber, *Director, Board on Science Education, National Academies of Sciences, Engineering, and Medicine*
Maya Garcia (*Chair*), *Colorado Department of Education*

11:15 am **Panel:** ***Centering Student Experience in Science***
Moderator: Ravit Duncan, *Rutgers University*
Virtual Moderator: Jessica Henderson-Rockette, *Instruction Partners*

Panelists:

- Rabiah Harris, *8th Grade Science Teacher, Ida B. Wells Middle School*
- Lauren Kaupp, *State of Hawaii Department of Education*
- Maria Olivares, *Boston University*
- Enrique Suárez, *University of Massachusetts, Amherst*
- Edna Tan, *University of North Carolina at Greensboro*

12:00 pm **Discussion/Q&A with panelists**

12:20 pm **Break**

1:00 pm **Presentation and Panel Discussion:** ***Teacher Professional Learning***

Moderators: Victor Sampson, *University of Texas at Austin* and Tricia Shelton, *National Science Teaching Association (NSTA)*

Virtual Moderators: Ravit Duncan, *Rutgers University* and James Blake, *Lincoln Public Schools*

1:00 pm **NSTA Survey:** ***Setting the Stage***

Overview presented by Tricia Shelton, *NSTA*

1:15 pm **Panel:** ***Teacher Educator Preparation***

Moderator: Victor Sampson, *University of Texas at Austin*

Panelists:

- Melissa Braaten, *University of Colorado Boulder*
- Lizette Burks, *University of Houston–Downtown*
- Todd Campbell, *University of Connecticut*
- Thomas Philip, *University of California, Berkeley*

1:55 pm **Discussion**

2:05 pm **Stretch Break**

2:15 pm **Panel:** ***Teacher Professional Development***

Moderator: Tricia Shelton, *NSTA*

Panelists:

- Jody Bintz, *BSCS Science Learning*
- K. Renae Pullen, *Caddo Parish Public Schools*
- Breigh Rhodes, *Louisiana Department of Education*
- Stacey van der Veen, *Leadership in Science, LLC*
- Julie Yu, *Exploratorium*

2:55 pm **Discussion**

3:05 pm **Discussion/Q&A across Both Panels**
Moderator: Victor Sampson, *University of Texas at Austin*

3:45 pm **Break**

4:00 pm **Open Discussion:** *Reflections on the day*
Facilitator: Maya Garcia, *Colorado Department of Education*

4:30 pm **Wrap up and Adjourn**
Maya Garcia (*Chair*), *Colorado Department of Education*

DAY 3: WEDNESDAY, DECEMBER 8TH

11:00 am **Welcome, Day 1 and 2 Overview and Day 3 Framing**
Maya Garcia (*Chair*), *Colorado Department of Education*

11:15 am **Panel: *Curriculum and Instructional Materials***
Moderator: Sam Shaw, *EdReports.org*
Virtual Moderator: Tricia Shelton, *NSTA*

Panelists:

- Philip Bell, *University of Washington*
- Cory Epler, *Nebraska Department of Education*
- Dora Kastel, *New Visions for Public Schools*
- Spencer Martin, *Kansas City Public Schools*
- Carol O'Donnell, *Smithsonian Science Education Center*
- Jamie Rumage, *Oregon Department of Education*

12:15 pm **Discussion/Q&A with panelists**

12:45 pm **Break**

1:15 pm **Panel:** ***Assessment as a "Caring Practice"—Systems of Assessment***

Moderator: Aneesha Badrinarayan, *Learning Policy Institute*
Virtual Moderator: Sam Shaw, *EdReports.org*

Panelists:

- Daniel Alcazar-Roman, formerly *DC Office of the State Superintendent of Education*
- Alec Barron, *San Diego Science Project*
- Tamara "TJ" Heck, *Michigan Department of Education*
- Angela Landrum, *Colorado Department of Education*
- Jim Pellegrino, *University of Illinois at Chicago*

2:00 pm **Discussion/Q&A with panelists**

2:30 pm **Break**

2:45 pm **Breakout Session:** ***What are the Tools and Resources that are Building Capacity and Driving Coherence?***

Activity: Participants will discuss the tools and resources that are building capacity and driving coherence with regard to standards implementation. In sessions, participants will consider areas for improvement of adaptation and consider emerging and urgent needs.

- **Group 1: Preschool to Elementary Transition**
- **Group 2: Curriculum and Instructional Materials**
- **Group 3: Formative Assessment**
- **Group 4: Instructional Practice**

3:45 pm **Break & Transition from Breakout Rooms**

4:00 pm **Breakout Group Report Out and Open Discussion**
Each group will report out the main ideas discussed in each breakout room.

Facilitator: Heidi Schweingruber, *Director, Board on Science Education*

- **Preschool to Elementary Transition Reporter:** Andres Bustamante, *University of California, Irvine*
- **Curriculum and Instructional Materials Reporter:** Christine Cunningham, *Pennsylvania State University*
- **Formative Assessment Reporter:** Sara Cooper, *Independent Consultant*
- **Instructional Practice Reporter:** Kate McNeill, *Boston College*

4:45 pm **Open Discussion:** *Reflections on the day*
Facilitator: Maya Garcia, *Colorado Department of Education*

5:00 pm **Wrap up and Adjourn**
Maya Garcia (*Chair*), *Colorado Department of Education*
Heidi Schweingruber, *Director, Board on Science Education*

Appendix B

Biographies of Committee Members and Presenters

DANIEL ALCAZAR-ROMAN (*Presenter*) is the associate director of the learning design group at the Lawrence Hall of Science at the University of California, Berkeley. Previously, he led the science assessment efforts at the state education agency in the District of Columbia. In that role, Alcazar-Roman led the design and implementation of a new state-level large-scale assessment based on the Next Generation Science Standards. As part of this effort he also launched a science assessment for students with significant cognitive disabilities. Prior to joining the DC government, he spent 12 years as a district science supervisor supporting schools in the Houston Independent School District in Texas and Alexandria City Public Schools in Virginia. During those years he gained extensive experience in the development of curriculum tools, assessments, and professional development opportunities in support of rigorous science teaching and learning. He started his education career as a bilingual science teacher and school administrator in downtown Houston. He holds a Bachelor of Science degree in engineering from Lipscomb University and an M.A. in education administration from Texas Southern University.

ANEESHA BADRINARAYAN (*Planning Committee Member*) supports Learning Policy Institute (LPI) projects related to performance assessments. For the past decade, her work has focused on supporting states, districts, and educators to develop and implement student-centered systems of assessment that support all learners. Prior to LPI, she was the Director for Special Initiatives at Achieve, a museum professional, and a neuroscientist. Her portfolio includes leading several multistate teams of leaders and experts to redefine "alignment" in the era of new state standards; developing criteria for innovative large-scale and classroom assessments; providing professional learning and strategic guidance for state leaders; and conducting analyses of state, local, and expert efforts to design and implement performance assessments and systems of assessment in science. Badrinarayan earned an M.S. in neuroscience at the University of Michigan, where she served as a research fellow for the National Institute of Mental Health, and a B.A. in biology from Cornell University.

ALEC BARRON (*Presenter*) is the director of the San Diego Science Project at the University of California, San Diego CREATE. Barron has worked to develop teachers, curriculum, and instructional practices that engage students in learning science. In his previous role as a science content specialist in Escondido Union High School District, he led the design of new curricula, professional learning events, and instructional coaching to support Next Generation Science Standards implementation. He has 13 years of experience as a teacher and taught a variety of science subjects from grades 6 through 12 at schools with culturally and socioeconomically diverse students. His experience in the classroom inspired him to complete a social justice-based Ed.D. in leadership for educational equity with the University of Colorado Denver. This graduate work supported his equity design work in grant funded projects like Competency X, an assessment practice for workforce informed performance tasks that was developed to broaden access to STEM college and career opportunities.

PHILIP BELL (*Presenter*) studies equitable science and STEM education in school and informal contexts. He is a professor of learning sciences and human development in the College of Education at the University of Washington where he holds the Shauna C. Larson Endowed Chair in Learning Sciences. His current research focuses on understanding and resourcing equity improvements in pre-K–12 science education—with a key focus on promoting climate and environmental justice across scales of educational implementation. Bell is a white settler scholar who has studied equitable approaches to science and engineering instruction, how people learn science and engineering across formal and informal environments, youth argumentation and conceptual change, culturally expansive and resurgent science instruction, scaled implementation of educational improvement, and how learning technologies support science learning. He has worked with families and communities in their home settings and neighborhoods, in classrooms and school districts, in informal education programs, and across school districts and national networks in partnership with educational leaders and teachers. He edits a National Science Foundation-funded educator resource collection called STEM Teaching Tools and has an academic background in human cognition and development, science education, computer science, and electrical engineering.

JODY BINTZ (*Presenter*) serves as BSCS Associate Director for Strategic Partnerships and Professional Learning and as co-director of the NEXUS Academy for Science Curriculum Leadership. She works primarily in the areas of leadership development and teacher professional learning. Bintz designs, studies, and leads programs to develop organizational leadership capacity, particularly as related to implementing the Next Generation Science Standards. Bintz serves as co-principal investigator of an efficacy study of the professional development program Science Teachers Learning from Lesson Analysis (STeLLA) and its impact on high school biology student learning and teacher practice. She also leads the professional learning and leadership development components of a study of STeLLA scale up and sustainability in grades 4 and 5 with partner organizations and schools from across Kentucky and Tennessee.

JAMES BLAKE (*Planning Committee Member*) is the Director of Strategic Initiatives and Focus Programs for Lincoln Public Schools (LPS) and the retiring president of the National Science Education Leadership Association (NSELA). Blake was previously the K–12 Science Curriculum Specialist for LPS and state science supervisor for Nebraska. His areas of expertise include working with community partners to develop new focus programs, and supporting existing Science and Arts and Humanities focus programs as principal. Blake previously worked with the National Academies of Sciences, Engineering, and Medicine on January 9–10, 2019, at the workshop "Realizing the Vision: NGSS District Implementation." As president-elect of NSELA, he presented at the workshop alongside other large national support organizations interested in helping districts implement Next Generation Science Standards (NGSS) and the *Framework*: Board on Science Education, Achieve, National Science Teaching Association, National Association for Research in Science Teaching, Council of State Science Supervisors, and American Association for the Advancement of Science. He earned his M.S., M.S.T., and Ed.D. in educational administration at the University of Nebraska–Lincoln.

MELISSA BRAATEN (*Presenter*) is an assistant professor of STEM education and teacher learning, research, and practice at the University of Colorado in Boulder. She taught upper elementary, middle, and high school science for 13 years. Her research focuses on the complexities of teaching science in culturally sustaining and responsive ways that advocate for justice. She is interested in how teaching is shaped by the political and institutional contexts of schools, education reforms, and education policy and how teachers' voices and experiences should be part of shaping those contexts. As a teacher educator and researcher, Braaten conducts research in long-term partnerships with teachers, schools, and systems examining teacher learning from preservice throughout the career trajectory.

LIZETTE BURKS (*Presenter*) taught middle and high school science in Texas and Kansas supporting schools with high percentages of learners impacted by poverty. In 2016, Burks joined the Kansas State Department of Education where she led the Department's state-wide implementation efforts around the Next Generation Science Standards advancing equity-focused innovations for pre-K–12 STEM education. Currently, she is an assistant professor of educational leadership at the University of Houston-Downtown, Texas. Burks' developing lines of research are motivated by learning English as a second language as a child and, later, committing to making learning more equitable for students from historically underserved communities. She has joined the University of Houston–Downtown to develop an M.A. degree in educational leadership focused on equity.

ANDRES BUSTAMANTE (*Presenter*) is an assistant professor at the University of California, Irvine's School of Education, and directs the Social, iTerative, Engaged, and Meaningful (STEM) Learning Lab. He designs and implements play-based early childhood STEM interventions in places and spaces that children and families spend time. He maintains an intentional focus on translating rigorous science from the lab into meaningful research in the classroom and the community. Bustamante is invested in research that has practical implications for school and life success for children and families from underserved communities. He is also committed to sharing and interpreting early childhood research with a broader audience through blog posts and other media outlets.

TODD CAMPBELL (*Presenter*) is the Department Head of Curriculum and Instruction and a professor of science education in the Neag School of Education. His research focuses on cultivating imaginative and equitable representations of STEM activity. This is accomplished in formal science learning environments through partnering with preservice and in-service science teachers and leaders to collaboratively focus on supporting student use of modeling as an anchoring epistemic practice to reason about events that happen in the natural world. This work extends into informal learning environments through a focus on iterative design of informal learning spaces and equity focused STEM identity research. He is currently the co-editor in chief of the *Journal of Science Teacher Education* and the co-principal investigator on National Science Foundation-funded projects focused on teacher education and informal science learning.

SARA COOPER (*Presenter*) is a dedicated science education leader who applies more than 15 years of experience as an educator—in formal and informal settings ranging from elementary to college-level—to her work developing creative solutions in educational systems. As a former state department of education science specialist, she has a deep understanding of the opportunities and challenges related to systemic and systematic educational change. Work in multiple roles has allowed her to evaluate and develop instructional materials, engage educators in high-quality professional learning experiences centered on instructional shifts and 5-D assessment, and coordinate science implementation within a variety of local and state system contexts. Cooper holds B.A. degrees in biological sciences and secondary education-natural sciences; an M.A. in teaching, learning, and teacher education; and an Ed.D. in educational studies, all from the University of Nebraska–Lincoln.

GUDIEL R. CROSTHWAITE (*Presenter*) is currently the superintendent at Lynwood Unified School District (LUSD) in the County of Los Angeles. Crosthwaite has enjoyed more than 25 years in education, including teaching, mentoring, and leadership focused on removing educational barriers. In 2013, as the assistant superintendent of educational services, his leadership team was instrumental in the District's extraordinary gains in achievement, including in graduation rates and enrollment in Advanced Placement (AP) coursework. LUSD was one of only three districts in the nation—and only one in California—to be named 2017 AP District of the Year by the College Board for its AP performance.

CHRISTINE CUNNINGHAM (*Presenter*) is the founding director of Youth Engineering Solutions, which develops equity-oriented, research-based, field-tested curricula and professional learning resources for preK–8 youth and their educators. Her research focuses on articulating frameworks for precollege engineering education and exploring affordances of engineering for learners. Her book, *Engineering in Elementary STEM Education*, describes her groundbreaking work in engineering education. Previously, Cunningham was a vice president at the Museum of Science in Boston where she founded Engineering is Elementary, which reached 200,000 educators and 20 million children under her leadership. Cunningham currently serves as a member of the National Assessment Governing Board and the chair of the National Academy of Engineering's Inclusive, Diverse, Equitable Engineering, for All Committee. She is a fellow of the American Society for Engineering Education and has received numerous awards including the American Society for Engineering Education K–12 and Pre-College Division Lifetime Achievement Award, the Institute of Electrical and Electronics Engineers Pre-University Educator Award, and the International Society for

Design and Development in Education Prize. Cunningham holds joint B.A. and M.A. degrees in biology from Yale University and a Ph.D. in education from Cornell University.

ELIZABETH A. (BETSY) DAVIS (*Presenter*) is a science educator and teacher educator at the University of Michigan. She is especially interested in beginning and experienced elementary teachers, teachers learning to engage in rigorous and consequential science teaching, and the roles of curriculum materials and practice-based teacher education in promoting teacher learning. She received the Presidential Early Career Award for Scientists and Engineers at the White House in 2002. She was a member of the National Research Council consensus committee that developed the report *Science Teachers' Learning* and the workshop planning committee on *Design, Selection, and Implementation of Instructional Materials for the Next Generation Science Standards* (*NGSS*). Most recently, she served as the chair of the National Academies of Sciences, Engineering, and Medicine consensus committee that developed the report *Science and Engineering in Preschool through Elementary Grades: The Brilliance of Children and the Strengths of Educators*. Davis received her Ph.D. from the University of California, Berkeley.

RAVIT GOLAN DUNCAN (*Planning Committee Member*) is a professor of learning sciences and science education with a joint appointment in the Graduate School of Education and the School of Environmental and Biological Sciences at Rutgers University. Duncan coordinates and teaches in the Certification Program in Biological Sciences at Rutgers University. Her current research focuses on two main strands: designing and studying of inquiry-based learning environments in sciences that foster epistemic reasoning through engagement with scientific practices; and studying learning progressions in science education, and specifically in genetics. Duncan has published in both education research journals and practitioner journals, and has co-edited the National Science Teachers Association Press book *Disciplinary Core Ideas: Reshaping Teaching and Learning*. She received her Ph.D. in learning sciences from Northwestern University.

CORY EPLER (*Presenter*) is the academic officer for the Nebraska Department of Education. As the academic officer, Epler provides strategic leadership, support, and coordination of activities, resources, and programs related to teaching, learning, and assessment in order to lead and support the preparation of all Nebraskans for learning, earning, and living.

ZOE EVANS (*Presenter*) is the principal of Bowdon High School in Bowdon, Georgia. Before becoming an administrator in 2012, she served as a middle grades science teacher for 19 years in both Florida and Georgia. Evans is a National Board Certified teacher in Early Adolescent Science and a Georgia Master Teacher. She is the 2005 Georgia recipient of the Presidential Award of Excellence in Mathematics and Science Teaching. Evans served as a member of the writing team for the Next Generation Science Standards (NGSS) and has collaborated on many projects including the NGSS EQuIP Professional Learning Facilitator's Guide, NGSS Example Bundles, and NGSS Evidence Statements. She also serves as an EQuIP Rubric Facilitator, a member of the National Science Teaching Association Professional Learning Cadre, and a member of the NextGen TIME network. She earned a B.A. in middle grades education, an M.A. degree in middle grades science, and a specialist's degree in middle grade science from the University of West Georgia. Additionally, she has received certification in educational leadership from the University of West Georgia.

MAYA M. GARCIA (*Planning Committee Chair*) joined the Colorado Department of Education (CDE) as the science content specialist in 2019, where she leads the implementation efforts for the newly adopted 2020 Colorado Academic Standards for Science and supports CDE's STEM education portfolio. Garcia began her career in science education as a middle school science teacher and science department chair, in the District of Columbia, where she taught for more than eight years. In 2013, she joined the District of Columbia Office of the State Superintendent of Education, where she led the District's adoption and implementation efforts around the Next Generation Science Standards, and Common Core Mathematics, and developed the District's plan for advancing pre-K–12 STEM education. Garcia has served on various national committees and boards including the National Academies of Sciences, Engineering, and Medicine's Board on Science Education and the Council of State Science Supervisors. She holds a B.S. in neuroscience and behavior from Mount Holyoke College and an M.A. in science teaching from American University, where she served as adjunct faculty in the School of Education, and is currently pursing her Ed.D. in leadership for educational equity at the University of Colorado, Denver.

RABIAH HARRIS (*Presenter*) teaches eighth-grade science in Washington, DC. She has taught and supported science instruction for 16 years in DC Public Schools (DCPS), a DC and New Orleans public charter school, and Pittsburgh Public Schools. Harris has taught a number of science courses and STEM electives from 6th grade to 12 grade. She also helped support the Next Generation Science Standards adoption in DCPS through training and course blueprint realignment.

TAMARA "TJ" HECK (*Presenter*) has been involved in *Framework*-based curriculum and assessment design since 2011. Currently, she is leading the development and implementation for Michigan's Next Generation Science Standards-aligned state summative science assessment. Through this process, Heck has designed professional learning for teacher/researcher teams to write item clusters for state summative use.

MICHAEL HEINZ (*Presenter*) serves as the science coordinator for the New Jersey Department of Education, a position that he has held for more than 16 years. His work focuses on academic standards and their implementation in K–12 public schools. He is currently the president of the Council of State Science Supervisors, a professional organization whose members have direct accountability to the state territorial agencies given the constitutional authority for education.

JESSICA HENDERSON-ROCKETTE (*Planning Committee Member*) currently serves as the director of science for Instruction Partners. She specializes in K–12 science education, specifically focused on building tools and processes for building long-lasting school leadership capacity that results in the successful adaptation and implementation of science instructional materials as a key lever for high-quality standard implementation. In her current work, she leads her organization's science research and development agenda to improve equitable access to high-quality science opportunities for all students. This agenda currently includes (1) the design, testing, and publication of a science instructional observational tool for diagnosing science instruction in classrooms and informing changes in instructional practice and (2) the formation and launch of a web-based Science Leader Development Series created to improve principals and other school leaders' ability to establish their own vision of excellent science instruction, speak to the conceptual shifts that ground the Next Generation Science Standards and similar science standards, and diagnose instruction while leading change in instructional practice in their own schools. She received her Ed.D. in educational leadership and policy studies from the University of Memphis.

DORA KASTEL (*Presenter*) is a curriculum development and professional learning manager for science at New Visions for Public Schools. She supports science teaching and learning in the New Visions network and beyond through the development of standards-aligned instructional materials along with facilitation of professional learning for both teachers and leaders. Kastel previously taught middle school science and math in East Harlem, and was a professional development provider at the American Museum of Natural History. While at the museum, her projects included the *Five Tools and Processes for Translating the NGSS Into Instruction and Class-*

room Assessment, the National Science Foundation-funded *Moving Next Generation Science Standards into Practice: A Middle School Ecology Unit and Teacher Professional Development Model*, and a Next Generation Science Standards (NGSS) video series with the Teaching Channel. Kastel holds a B.A. in geology from the University of Pennsylvania, and M.A. and Ed.M. degrees in science and mathematics education from Teachers College, Columbia University, and is currently working on her Ph.D. in science education.

LAUREN KAUPP (*Presenter*) is the science specialist for the State of Hawai'i Department of Education, where her work is centered on supporting Next Generation Science Standards-aligned teaching and learning, and providing leadership in science and STEM education state initiatives. Prior to this position, she designed curriculum and developed and facilitated professional learning for teachers in marine science and physics at the University of Hawai'i at Mānoa. She also taught high school chemistry and physics at a public charter school in Hawai'i. She holds a B.S. in chemistry from the University of Maryland, Baltimore County, an M.S. in oceanography (chemical) from the University of Hawai'i at Mānoa, and an Ed.D. in educational leadership from the University of Southern California.

MICHAEL LACH (*Presenter*) is the Assistant Superintendent for Curriculum, Instruction, and Assessment at Township High School District 113, a small school district on the outside of Chicago. Lach began his professional career teaching high school biology and general science at Alceé Fortier Senior High School in New Orleans in 1990 as a charter member of Teach For America. In 2009, he was appointed by Secretary Arne Duncan to lead science and mathematics education efforts at the U.S. Department of Education. Starting in 2013, he led a variety of research and technical assistance projects focusing on large-scale improvements in mathematics and science education as the Director of STEM Education and Strategic Initiatives at UChicago STEM Education at the University of Chicago. As a senior fellow at Achieve from 2016 to 2019, he led all content-related work, including standards work in mathematics, science, and English language arts. He earned a B.S. in physics from Carleton College, M.A. degrees from Columbia University and Northeastern Illinois University, and a doctorate from the University of Illinois at Chicago.

ANGELA LANDRUM (*Presenter*) has, for more than 13 years, served as the Principal Consultant for Assessment Systems at the Colorado Department of Education. She led the design and implementation of the 2009 Colorado Academic Standards revision process, served as the facilitator of the Interim and Formative Assessment Subcommittee during the state's

2010 assessment system revision, and led the Colorado Race to the Top Program. In 2013, she led the development of the Colorado Assessment Literacy Program, which includes online professional learning modules, formative assessment supports, and a workshop series on developing high-quality classroom assessments. Currently she is leading the development of the performance assessment component of the Colorado Graduation Guidelines Menu of Assessment Options. Landrum has been in the classroom at the preschool, high school, and university levels, and has served in executive leadership roles in the university and nonprofit sectors. She holds a B.A. from Loyola Marymount University and an M.A. from the University of California, Los Angeles.

STEFANIE L. MARSHALL (*Presenter*) is an assistant professor at the University of Minnesota–Twin Cities. Marshall has worked as a middle and high school science teacher as well as a district manager for an educational service provider in districts across the State of Michigan. Marshall does not take her intersectional identity as a Black woman who is a doer of science for granted. She strives to engage key decision makers and policy makers to disrupt the status quo of limited opportunities for marginalized youth to engage in the sciences. Marshall situates her work at the intersection of educational policy, leadership, and science education, focusing on the systemic and organizational needs for science education. Marshall researches (1) ways to support equity in science/STEM education through building and sustaining networks, (2) the impact of policies on science/STEM education, and (3) the role of school administrators in science/STEM education.

SPENCER MARTIN (*Presenter*) attended Texas Tech University for his undergraduate teacher preparation and then joined the Peace Corps and taught science in Malawi, Africa. Directly after the Peace Corps, Martin moved to Austin to work in Austin Independent School District (ISD) and then Manor ISD at Manor New Technology High School. While at Manor New Tech, Martin completed his M.A. in STEM education: engineering at University of Texas, Austin. He then worked for a short time at an education technology startup in downtown Austin before moving to Kansas City, Kansas, for his current role as the Lead Secondary Science Curriculum Instructional Coach for Kansas City, Kansas, Public Schools. While in Kansas City, Martin completed his Ed.S. degree in curriculum and instruction at the University of Missouri, Kansas City.

KATHERINE L. McNEILL (*Presenter*) is a professor of science education at Boston College. A former middle school science teacher, she received her doctorate in science education from the University of Michigan. Her research focuses on how to support students with diverse backgrounds in engaging in science practices as they make sense of phenomena. She has worked on projects designing and researching curriculum, assessments, professional development, and other resources to support students, teachers, and instructional leaders in scientific sensemaking. Currently, she is leading the development of both teacher and facilitator professional learning materials for OpenSciEd, which provides high-quality open-source Next Generation Science Standards-aligned instructional materials.

ELIZABETH MULKERRIN (*Presenter*) is the Vice President of Education at the Omaha Zoo and Aquarium and the National Science Teaching Association (NSTA) president elect. In this position, Mulkerrin creates and designs zoo exhibits and associated educational materials, works to provide positive visitor experiences, partners with local leaders to engage the community, develops unique partnerships to drive the zoo's mission, developed a five-year strategic plan for the zoo, and raises funds through donors and corporate relations. She leads the team that provides quality STEM education programming to 158,000 students annually and is co-founder of the Omaha STEM Ecosystem, a grassroots organization that brings business and education together in developing Omaha's STEM workforce. In addition to her position on the NSTA Executive Board as president elect, Mulkerrin also served on the executive board and as president of the National Science Education Leadership Association (NSELA). She served as division director for informal science for both the NSTA and NSELA Board of Directors. She also completed the Association of Zoos and Aquariums Executive Leadership Development Certificate Program in 2019. She received her M.A. and Ph.D. degrees at the University of Nebraska at Omaha.

TIFFANY NEILL (*Presenter*) is the deputy superintendent of curriculum and instruction for the Oklahoma State Board of Education and the past-president for the Council of State Science Supervisors, an organization comprised of state leaders for science education. Neill serves as co-principal investigator for the National Science Foundation (NSF)-funded Advancing Coherent and Equitable Systems of Science Education project and is a member of the NSF STEM Advisory Panel and board member for Carnegies OpenSciEd Project and EdReports for Science. Prior to her current role, Neill served as the Executive Director of Curriculum and Instruction for three years and as the Director of Science and Engineering Education for five years at the Oklahoma State Department of Education. She began her career in education as a middle and high school teacher. She served on the National Academies of Sciences, Engineering, and Medicine consensus committee that authored the reports *Changing Expectations for the K–12 Teacher Workforce: Policies, Preservice Education, Professional Development, and the Workplace* and *Science and Engineering in*

Preschool through Elementary Grades: The Brilliance of Children and the Strengths of Educators. Neill is completing a Ph.D. in instructional leadership and academic curriculum in science education at the University of Oklahoma.

TAUNYA NESIN (*Presenter*) is a senior program officer at the Bill & Melinda Gates Foundation. At the foundation, her portfolio includes organizations that specialize in supporting the development and sustainment of coherent instructional systems. Prior experience includes accountability work at the DC Public Charter School Board and policy research at The George Washington University. Her primary research investigated how principals use evidence from research practice partnerships to inform decision making. She was an editor at the National Science Teaching Association, National Geographic School Publishing, and Houghton Mifflin Harcourt where she developed curricula for science and English language arts. Nesin started her career as a public school teacher in Hoboken, Atlanta, and Boston. She earned her B.A. from Harvard University, her M.A. in curriculum and instruction from Columbia University, Teachers College, and her Ed.D. in educational administration and policy Studies from The George Washington University.

CAROL O'DONNELL (*Presenter*) is senior executive and director of Smithsonian Science Education Center, dedicated to transforming K–12 education through science in collaboration with communities across the globe. O'Donnell's career spans being a K–8 science teacher, curriculum developer, research scientist for the Institute of Education Sciences, group leader at the U.S. Department of Education Office of State Support, and adjunct faculty for George Washington University's physics department. She serves on numerous STEM committees, including FC-STEM of the White House Office of Science and Technology Policy and the UN Broadband Commission Working Group on Digital Learning. Through a National Academies of Sciences, Engineering, and Medicine appointment, O'Donnell represents the United States on the Science Education Programme Global Council of the InterAcademy Partnership, the global network of 143 national academies. She is a member of the Council of State Science Supervisors and the International Dialogue on STEM Education, where she co-authored the position paper on STEM Education for Sustainable Development.

MARIA C. OLIVARES (*Presenter*) is a research assistant professor at the Earl Center for Learning and Innovation in Boston University's Wheelock College of Education and Human Development. Olivares designs learning environments and experiences that locate creativity and nurturance as a foundation and a product of expansive STEM-learning. Originally from

South Central Los Angeles, Olivares is the proud daughter of Mexican immigrants and the first in her family to gain access to higher education. In her research, she collaborates with youth, teachers, and other researchers to co-design learning settings that elevate creative and critical inquiry in science and computational thinking, with a commitment to transforming educational opportunities for youth and communities of color.

TAKAKO OLSON (*Presenter*) is the director of curriculum and instruction for Lincoln Public Schools in Lincoln, Nebraska. Growing up as a student in Tokyo, as well as being an elementary teacher and a high school administrator in the Unites States, her experience in education is versatile. Her area of expertise and interests include the intersectionality of being a woman and of color, intercurricular connections, equitable teaching practices and mindset, and implementation of curriculum and instruction in K–12 public school systems. She has earned her M.Ed., Ed.S., and Ed.D. from Doane University in Nebraska.

JAMES W. PELLEGRINO (*Presenter*) is Liberal Arts and Sciences Distinguished Professor and founding co-director of the Learning Sciences Research Institute at the University of Illinois at Chicago. He studies children's and adult's thinking and learning and the implications of research and theory for assessment and instructional practice. He has chaired several National National Research Council study committees that have issued major reports related to teaching, learning, and assessment, including the Committee for the Evaluation of the National and State Assessments of Educational Progress, the Committee on Learning Research and Educational Practice, and the Committee on the Foundations of Assessment. Most recently he served on the Committee on Science Learning: Games, Simulations and Education and the Committee on a Conceptual Framework for New Science Education Standards. He chaired the Committee on Defining Deeper Learning and 21st Century Skills, and co-chaired the Committee on Developing Assessments of Science Proficiency in K–12. He is a lifetime National Associate of the National Academy of Sciences and a past member of the Board on Testing and Assessment of the National Research Council. He is also a lifetime elected member of the National Academy of Education and the American Academy of Arts and Sciences.

BILL PENUEL (*Presenter*) is Distinguished Professor of Learning Sciences and Human Development in the School of Education and Institute of Cognitive Science at the University of Colorado Boulder. He designs and studies curriculum materials, assessments, and professional learning experiences for teachers in science. He works in partnership with school districts and state departments of education, and the research he conducts is in support of educational equity in three dimensions: (1) equitable implementation of new science standards; (2) creating inclusive classroom cultures that attend to students' affective experiences and where all students have authority for constructing knowledge together; and (3) connecting teaching to the interests, experiences, and identities of learners. Penuel is a member of the National Academy of Education and is a fellow of the International Society of the Learning Sciences, the International Society for Design and Development in Education, and the American Educational Research Association. He received his B.A. from Clark University in psychology, his Ed.M. in counseling processes from Harvard University, and his Ph.D. in developmental psychology from Clark University.

THOMAS M. PHILIP (*Presenter*) is a professor in the Graduate School of Education at University of California, Berkeley, where he also serves as the faculty director of teacher education. Philip's research focuses on how teachers make sense of power and hierarchy in classrooms, schools, and society. He is interested in how teachers act on their sense of agency as they navigate and ultimately transform classrooms and institutions toward more equitable, just, and democratic practices and outcomes. His recent scholarship explores the possibilities and tensions that emerge with the use of artificial intelligence, data analytics, and digital learning technologies in the classroom, particularly discourses about the promises of these tools with respect to the significance or dispensability of teacher pedagogy.

K. RENAE PULLEN (*Presenter*) is the elementary science curriculum instructional specialist for Caddo Parish Public Schools in Shreveport, Louisiana, and she is a member of the Caddo Teaching Academy faculty. Prior to being a science specialist, she was an elementary classroom teacher for 16 years. Pullen has received numerous awards including the Wal-Mart Local Teacher of the Year, Caddo Parish Teacher of the Year, Greater Shreveport and Bossier Chamber of Commerce's 40 Under 40 Honoree, and the Presidential Award for Excellence in Math and Science Teaching. Pullen has elevated the profession by serving on several local, state, and national committees; presenting at numerous workshops, webinars, and conferences; and serving as a member of the Board on Science Education for the National Academies of Sciences, Engineering, and Medicine. Pullen was a consulting expert for the National Academies practitioner's guide *Seeing Students Learn Science: Integrating Assessment and Instruction in the Classroom,* and served on the committees that produced *English Learners in STEM Subjects: Transforming Classrooms, Schools, and Lives* and *Science and Engineering in Preschool Through Elementary Grades: The Brilliance of Children and the Strengths of Educators.*

BREIGH RAINEY RHODES (*Presenter*) is the director of mathematics, science, and STEM at the Louisiana Department of Education. Rhodes serves Louisiana's 800,000+ students by ensuring teachers, schools, and systems have access to high-quality math, science, and STEM instructional materials and aligned professional development. Prior to joining the Department, Rhodes taught math and science and worked to support fellow educators through curriculum writing, teacher training, and STEM program innovation in Louisiana's public schools. Rhodes has earned several honors and awards for her work in STEM education, including the Essie Beck Rising Star Award, the Disney Planet Challenge Grand Prize, a National Geographic Grosvenor Fellowship, and the Council for Elementary Science International Muriel Green Award. Rhodes holds a B.S. in elementary education from Southeastern Louisiana University and an M.Ed. in gifted education from Louisiana State University.

JAMIE RUMAGE (*Presenter*) serves as the science education specialist at the Oregon Department of Education. In her role, she strives to elevate educational equity by supporting a statewide science education system that intentionally broadens the participation and engagement of all students. She develops science policy, practices, and procedures that build affirming science classrooms that harness students' culture, linguistic diversity, interests, and knowledge. She continues to coordinate these efforts through the implementation of the Next Generation Science Standards to advance high-quality science education. She currently serves as the First Year Director on the Council of State Science Supervisors (CSSS) Board and served as a co-chair of the Access and Equity Ad Hoc Committee, co-leading the development of the CSSS Position Statement on Equity and Access to Science Education. She holds a B.S in environmental education from Western Illinois University and an M.S. in science education from Oregon State University.

VICTOR SAMPSON (*Planning Committee Member*) examines how culturally and linguistically diverse groups of students participate in the practices of science, engineering, and mathematics and how to organize the interactions that take place among students, materials, and ideas in ways that promote and support learning. His current work focuses on the ways culturally and linguistically diverse groups of students support, evaluate, and revise ideas when attempting to develop explanations or solutions to problems; group and individual meaning-making during episodes of argumentation; the development of innovative instructional materials and strategies, and how to support teachers in making classroom instruction more equitable and inclusive. He has received several awards for his scholarship, including the 2008 National Association for Research in Science Teaching Outstanding Dissertation award and the 2012 National Association for Research in Science Teaching Early Career award.

JENNY SARNA (*Presenter*) directs NextGenScience, providing leadership and vision for the project's work supporting science educators and leaders nationwide. She assists district and agency leaders with planning, implementing, and evaluating science education programs—paying special attention to equity and access. Prior to joining WestEd, Sarna served as Achieve's director of district support, overseeing strategic planning initiatives that brought district-level leaders together to implement college and career-ready STEM policies. Sarna also led Chicago Public Schools' Next Generation Science Standards implementation strategy, as the district's high school science specialist and preK–12 science manager, where she built strategies focused on professional learning and external partnerships, strengthened graduation requirements, and oversaw the development and adoption of new K–8 science instructional materials. Sarna began her career teaching middle school and high school science, in Hidalgo, Mexico, and Chicago. Sarna graduated from the University of Notre Dame with a B.S.. She earned an M.A. in teaching from University of Chicago and an M.A. in educational studies from University of Illinois at Chicago.

HEIDI SCHWEINGRUBER (*Presenter*) is the director of the Board on Science Education at the National Academies of Sciences, Engineering, and Medicine. She oversees a portfolio of work that includes K–12 science education, informal science education, and higher education. Schweingruber joined the staff of the board in 2004 as a senior program officer. In this role, she directed or co-directed several projects including the study that resulted in the report *A Framework for K–12 Science Education*, the blueprint for the Next Generation Science Standards. Schweingruber is a nationally recognized leader in leveraging research findings to catalyze improvements in science and STEM education policy and practice. She holds a Ph.D. in psychology (developmental) and anthropology from the University of Michigan.

SAM SHAW (*Planning Committee Member*) is the director of science review at EdReports.org. Shaw came to EdReports from the South Dakota Department of Education, where he oversaw science education in addition to social studies, fine arts, advanced placement, the South Dakota Virtual School, among other programs, and was also a participant in the SD Governor's Leadership Program. He worked statewide with teachers and school leadership to advance education related to college and career readiness (CCR), specifically with regard to CCR standards implementation. Prior to his role at the Department of Education, Shaw was a middle school science teacher. He has also held positions of board director and financial officer with the Council of State Science Supervisors where he was also a collaborator on the Science Professional Learning Standards. He earned his B.S. in biology from South Dakota State University and his executive M.P.A. from the University of South Dakota.

TRICIA SHELTON (*Planning Committee Member*) worked with Kentucky students for 22 years as a middle school and high school science teacher and teacher leader. Shelton is a 2014 National Science Teaching Association (NSTA) Distinguished Teaching Award winner for her contributions to and demonstrated excellence in science teaching. She served as an EQuIP trainer for Achieve and a professional learning designer and facilitator for many organizations before joining the NSTA team. At NSTA, she is the chief learning officer and in that capacity works to support educators and students across the country as they work to integrate contemporary research in science education into classroom teaching and learning.

JAMES P. SPILLANE (*Presenter*) is the Spencer T. and Ann W. Olin Professor in Learning and Organizational Change at the School of Education and Social Policy at Northwestern University. A former primary school teacher at St. Mary's on the Hill N.S., Cork, Spillane has published extensively on issues of education policy, policy implementation, school reform, and school leadership. His work explores the policy implementation process at the state, district, school, and classroom levels, focusing on intergovernmental and policy-practice relations. He also studies organizational leadership and change, and distributed leadership in schools. Recent projects include studies of relations between organizational infrastructure and instructional advice-seeking in schools and the socialization of new school principals. Spillane is member of the National Academy of Education and the American Academy of Arts and Sciences.

ENRIQUE (HENRY) SUÁREZ (*Presenter*) is an assistant professor of science education at University of Massachusetts, Amherst. He is committed to making science learning equitable for students and teachers, emphasizing the importance of knowing about the natural world through investigation. Drawing on a range of learning theories, Suárez works in partnership with K–12 schools and communities to make science learning more equitable for learners from historically underserved communities. Suárez has extensive experience teaching elementary science methods courses, co-designing and co-facilitating professional development for K–12 science teachers, and developing physics-based K–12 curriculum. He is an astrophysicist who did cosmology research for five years before choosing a career in K–5 science education. He holds a B.S. in astrophysics from the University of Oklahoma, an M.S. in science education from Tufts University, and a Ph.D. on curriculum and instruction—science education from the University of Colorado, Boulder.

EDNA TAN (*Presenter*) is professor of science education at the University of North Carolina at Greensboro. Her collaborative research investigates the design, support, and outcomes of equitable and consequential STEM learning for historically minoritized youth across learning contexts and over time. Current National Science Foundation-funded projects include longitudinal, community-engaged research with minoritized and refugee youth engaging in makerspace work, focused on identifying the elements of an authentic, community-owned, and youth-centered making space; and working with middle school teachers in co-developing and enacting an engineering for sustainable communities curriculum that attends to students' identity work and engineering toward justice-oriented ends. Tan is a fellow of the American Association for the Advancement of Science.

STACEY (GRUBER) VAN DER VEEN (*Presenter*) has extensive experience designing and delivering professional development programs to support New Jersey school districts as they implement the Next Generation Science Standards (NGSS). She spends much of her time in schools working elbow-to-elbow with teams of teachers as they implement the vision behind the NGSS in their classrooms. She also works with science coaches and administrators, building their leadership skills for supporting science teachers. Before founding Leadership in Science, van der Veen was the manager of education programs for the Merck Institute for Science Education, a nationally recognized nonprofit organization dedicated to improving science teaching and learning in public schools. She started her career teaching science and mathematics at high schools in Newark, New Jersey, and New York City and has more than 20 years of K–12 teaching and administrative experience in both public and private schools. She co-founded the Hoboken Charter School, one of the first cohort of schools chartered in New Jersey, where she served as co-principal and child study team coordinator. She earned her Ed.M. in secondary science education from the Harvard Graduate School of Education and her B.A. in biology from the University of Pennsylvania.

JULIE YU (*Presenter*) is a senior scientist at the Exploratorium, San Francisco's museum of science, art, and human perception. She provides science content support throughout the museum and works with teachers to bring inquiry-based science learning to their classrooms as part of the Exploratorium's Teacher Institute, a nationally recognized teacher professional learning center. With broad interests in science and education, her research has spanned from viruses and stem cells to teacher learning and inquiry to concrete and cement. This has led to a myriad of opportunities, including teaching science to Tibetan monks and nuns, launching an explosion of 2,000 ping pong balls, and acquiring a U.S. patent. Yu holds a B.S. in chemical engineering from Brown University and a Ph.D. in chemical engineering with a minor in molecular and cell biology from the University of California, Berkeley.